THE MAKING OF A MORON

By

NIALL
BRENNAN

THE ✓ 230

MAKING

OF

A

MORON

SHEED ✓
AND
WARD
NEW YORK

COPYRIGHT BY SHEED AND WARD, INC.

NEW YORK 1953

MANUFACTURED IN THE U.S.A.

LIBRARY OF CONGRESS CATALOG NO. 53—9632

There goes the happy moron
He doesn't give a dam';
I wish I were a moron.
My God! Perhaps I am.

Author unknown

My thanks are due to B. A. Santamaria, Director of Catholic Action, Melbourne, Australia, who first suggested the line of enquiry which led to this book; to Miss Mary Todd, M.Sc., who advised me on some scientific matters; to Joe Mearns and Edward Petraki, both Christian business-men who told me some of the facts I used; and to my patient wife Elaine, who read the MS., clarified it, and corrected it.

N.B.

Epiphany, 1952

To

F. J. S. AND M. W.

in gratitude

CONTENTS

CONTENTS

conclusion relat. to Labor & - quality + pack-cle of labour
describe the author. i'nroads
basic thrust: of production

vague in actually
about thesis
assessing why he considers the
skilled to be

say only
or — millionares never had
anyway the real
selve wanted.
unleashes at end:
r 156
spiritual
becomes philosophical

I

THE USE OF MORONS

THE DIRECTOR of Mental Hygiene in Victoria, Australia—Dr. Catarinich—wanted to find out whether there was any way in which the subnormals under his care could be put into useful work. On the face of it, it seemed difficult to find openings in normal employment and sane society for those afflicted members of it who had been banished for lack of full mental ability. The duty of the Department however was not only to cure but also to rehabilitate. It had to explore possibilities; and in this case, the face of industry, which seemed so unpromising, turned out to be a mask. Dr. Catarinich found that there were very few industrial occupations beyond the ability of subnormals. Furthermore, the problem had been faced and partly solved overseas. In 1917, for example, the New York State textile factories had been short of labour. There was a state of war, business was brisk, but manpower was precious. The Utica Knitting Mill made an arrangement with the Rome Institution for Mentally Defective Girls, and a house was purchased next to the Utica plant at Oriskanny Falls. The mill rented the house to the institution, and twenty-four girls whose mental ages ranged from six to ten years were placed in it and put to work at the mill.

Nobody thought that the girls would be as competent as their "normal" working companions. But in a war emergency, the Utica mill was prepared to put up with the next best thing. The conventions of business allowed the use of cheap female labour in peacetime, so the use of subnormals in wartime was not questioned. But the little morons surprised them, and the Company kept them in employment long after the war emergency ended. It also asked the institution to establish similar hostels near plants at Richfield Springs and Clayville. These housed forty girls in each, and apart from a few house-girls, all worked in the Company's factories. They were fully, wholly and congenially employed. They were themselves extremely happy, and they rattled through their work with the dexterity of veterans. Not only their working companions, who laboured under the apparent disadvantage of enjoying full mental stature, but also the managers were surprised at how efficient they were.

The managers were not, of course, concerned with experiments in mental readjustment. That was the institution's affair. The managers were only interested in production, and their unqualified praise of the sub-normal girls is free from any taint of academic bias. In several important reports, they said that "when business conditions required a reduction of the working staff", the hostel girls were never "laid off" in disproportion to the normal girls; that the behaviour of the subnormals was "better" than that of the normal girls; that they were more punctual, more regular in their habits, and did not indulge in as much "gossip and levity". They received the same rate of pay, and they had been employed successfully at almost every process carried out in the workshops.

In 1928, the Clayville and Oriskanny Mills closed, but the plant at Richfield Springs and its hostel were still working in 1940, about the time the Australian Department decided to carry out some experiments of its own. From its Travancore School for Mentally Deficient Children, it took five young morons, placed them in a special hostel, and sent them out to work for Radio Corporation Ltd., a large plant mass-producing electrical and radio goods.

Four weeks after the experiment started, in February 1941, the Works Manager of R.C.A. wrote to the Department and said:

> . . . the three girls compared very favourably with the normal class of employee in that age group. The boy employed in the store performed his work with satisfaction. . . . Although there was some doubt about the fifth child, it was felt that getting the most out of him was just a matter of right placement.

In each of the five cases, the morons were reported to be quiet, respectful, well-behaved, and very obedient. The Works Manager was especially impressed by their "truthfulness, and the lack of deceit or suppression of the facts".

These children were selected samples of subnormality from the higher to the lower borderline, and a wide variation of individual skill was expected. The lowest grade child, the boy whose efficiency was just a matter of "right placement", suffered from physical disabilities which interfered with muscular co-ordination. Of him the Chief Psychiatrist at Travancore submitted a jubilant report to his Director in which he said:

If the Works Manager is confident that so poor an industrial proposition as this boy can be adapted to some of their processes, it is safe to say that the vast majority of the mentally handicapped can be transformed into effective process workers.

Three months later, the Medical Superintendent of Travancore announced that

. . . Their services are still satisfactory and this is borne out by the frequency with which bonuses are paid to them.

A year later, the same Works Manager was still able to advise Travancore that

In every case, these girls proved to be exceptionally well-behaved, particularly obedient, and strictly honest and trustworthy. They carried out work required of them to such a degree of efficiency that *we were surprised they were classed as subnormals* for their age. Their attendance was good, and their behaviour was, if anything, certainly better than any other employee of the same age [my emphasis].

The scheme was enlarged. More girls were put with Radio Corporation, and in 1942 ten girls were sent to a new hostel at Daylesford, and there employed by Day-Tex Fabrics. Day-Tex was enthusiastic." The first four ", wrote their spokesman, "from our (i.e. production) point of view, in intellect and ability to perform their work are at least equal to, and in many cases better than, our 'normal' [his inverted commas] girls. . . . Generally speaking, we are very satisfied with these girls as a whole."

These reports are not a full account of all the experiments in industrial readjustment on subnormals. But they are significant. Two high-ranking business executives had expressed surprise that these girls were even classed as subnormals. The Day-Tex manager did not have a high opinion at all of the girls he employed. Not only were the subnormals just as good as workers, they were equally intelligent.

The satisfaction of the Department is understandable. Its object was to find social outlets for mentally defective people. It was looking for work which would give to the defective his economic independence, and more important still, would lessen the sense of inferiority from which every defective suffers when he is unable to do himself the common tasks of others about him. Nothing hurts subnormals more, nothing confirms them in their helplessness more, than having constantly to be helped by others. Nothing isolates them so much in the dim world of their imbecility more than the awareness of their own incomprehensible disability. The Department wanted work for them which would give them a place in the social order, a place of responsibility, a place* where they would not be different from but the same as their fellow-workers. And economically it wanted work for them, because they would then cease to be waste personnel dependent on charity, and could make their own contribution to the wealth of the community. This was the work it had found for them. Their pleasure was justified.

But the excellence of this is double-edged. If equality is established between two otherwise unequal elements, it does not necessarily mean that the worse has risen to the level of the better. Most revolutions designed to uplift the underdog have shown only too pathetically how much easier it is to pull down the topdog instead. There is something like the law of gravity in social relations. If equality is all that is aimed at, it is almost invariably achieved on the lower rather than the higher level. And when equality has been established, we must ask on whose level, before the celebrations can begin. When morons can be fitted into industry on an immediate parity with the normal employees, the question, on whose level this equality has been achieved, must also be asked. It may be good to discover that in a modern industrial plant there are conventional processes which can be performed by a boy with a mental age of less than eight years, and a severe lack of muscular co-ordination. It may be fine for the boy. But what were the "normal" adults doing in this same process before the crippled and retarded boy came along to do it for them? No really normal person can afford to ignore the frightening implications in the discovery that many "normal" men and women are working in jobs at which subnormals are equally and sometimes more efficient.

The achievements of subnormals can, in certain cases, be a tribute to their teachers rather than evidence of the simple nature of the process. Three surveys made during the 1920's showed a surprising number of trades, crafts, and arts which subnormals could be taught, with patience and understanding. This occupational therapy and rehabilitative training are always a part of skilled institutional care of the defective. But a circus elephant can be taught to play cricket, and it is nothing to do with this issue that a subnormal can be taught to play the bass horn. Such things demonstrate only the art of teaching; but the only teachers at Rome, Travancore and Daylesford were the foremen. The girls needed hardly more training than their "normal" companions. They fitted in promptly, neatly and immediately, and once in they were almost indistinguishable from their companions.

The Rome Institution experiments with what is called technically "the Social Control of the Mentally Defective" are among the earliest to reveal the nature of modern industrial processes; and the problem of industrial processes has been worrying a lot of people. One optimist, Mr. Arthur Otis ("Selection of Mill Workers by Mental Test"), tried to argue that industrial efficiency would improve if only the brightest available employees were hired. He actually began to sift out—by mental test—the duller from the more intelligent, but by the time he had sifted out three hundred employees whose record was known, he was obliged to announce sadly that he had found "no correlation between the mental age as measured by the test, and the ability to perform the work well".

Other reports are worth quoting. In Davies and Williams' *Social Control of the Mentally Deficient* (Constable, 1930), a work recommended by the Victoria Department of Mental Hygiene, the following conclusion is offered:

It may be said in all truth that many of the intellectually subnormal have a definite, even an important, place in society. There are numerous tasks in the world of the dull, monotonous, or routine type that can be better performed as a day-in, day-out proposition by the so-called subnormal. Psychological examination of factory employees has shown that some of the best operatives are mentally deficient. They are the steady plodding faithful workers who can best withstand the humdrum toil of machine work. A large firm in New York, after experimenting with its messenger service, came to the conclusion that the subnormal youth made the best messenger because he was most likely to be the most faithful in his attendance to his duties, and was content to hold his position longer than the normal boy.

Mr. Arthur Pound, who wrote *The Iron Man in Industry* discussed the same problem.

"The Iron Man" (i.e. the big machine) does not get on the nerves of those below average mentality. He is a consistent friend to the mentally defective. Just as deafness is an advantage in certain industrial occupations—our shops employ many mutes with satisfaction both ways—so mental lacks may become assets for certain industrial purposes. Given enough sense to master certain routine occupations and enough appreciation of duty or fear of relatives to come to the shop daily, the below-average person can soon be adjusted industrially. And when adjusted, the moron will be found immune to many of the pricks which irritate the normal man into seeing red, less fretted by monotony, less worn by rhythmic clatter. There is less in his soul striving to release itself. He has brought into the shop comparatively little that the shop cannot use. And so he accepts dumbly his appointed place in the scheme of things industrial, remains unbitten by ambition and reacts not at all against subordination. The less mind one has, the less it resents that invasion of personality which is inseparable from large scale or mechanised enterprises. I have heard industrial engineers and welfare workers say that industrial efficiency as working out in our day puts a premium on mental deficiency.

Mr. Ethelbert Stewart, Commissioner of the U.S. Bureau of Labour Statistics, adds this testament to the arrival of Mr. Aldous Huxley's *Brave New World:*

Personnel managers of textile mills took the view that textile mills formerly were operated by children and they saw no reason why adults of childlike intelligence should not do perfectly acceptable work. And after experiment, they reported that they did. Then along comes the automatic machinery which accomplishes mass production. We are told that "it is of course fortunate that a great many jobs made no particular call on mental alertness because this fact gives even dull minds a chance to find assignments at profitable jobs." Today we find the literature of efficiency and industrial managers full of suggestions as to the preferability of the employment of those men and women with a mental age of ten or less.

If certain premises are accepted, then this narrative should thrill the hearts of all men. The premises are that efficient industrial production is a primary virtue and that the material wealth of society and man is the only goal of society and man. I do not accept either of these premises. Wealth is not the end of man, nor therefore is industrial efficiency a major virtue. In fact, material wealth pursued as a goal in itself is harmful to the nature of man. So, therefore, industrial efficiency pursued as a means to this end without reference to true ends or moral means is harmful to the nature of man. But of this, more is said further on. The important point at this stage is that these premises, the virtue so-called of efficiency, and the end so-pursued of wealth, carried logically to their natural conclusions, are creating a situation where morons and subnormals might have more value than sane men. That is a moronic state of affairs. It does not seem to me to demonstrate progress of any sort.

THE USE OF MORONS

If it were simply a matter of finding work for morons, then of course there would be cause for general jubilation. But every further item of evidence produced illuminates another and more sinister implication. Davies and Williams (supra) give a hint of what it is.

> The mentally deficient, who by reason of dependency or delinquency, have come to public attention and have added to the problem of feeble-mindedness, are a small proportion only of the large numbers of mentally deficient persons who are more or less regularly employed for wages, lead uneventful lives, and live decently and happily in their own limited ways.

After all, two industrial managers said they could see no real difference between the trained morons supplied to them and their "normal" staff, except that generally the morons were better. Well, does it matter? Does it matter how many on the pay-roll of a knitting mill are morons? Does it matter whether they are under supervision or not so long as they are "usefully" employed? Yes, it does matter, a great deal.

There was a man named J. whose life in every outward respect was normal. He had a steady job, a wife and a family. He seemed happy and unambitious, and he plodded faithfully through a vegetable, but "socially useful" life. He read the papers, and in them the advertisements. He took his standard of morality unquestioningly from the films and the weekly magazines. He was subjected without relief to the continual proposition that his status as a human being would be raised if he became the owner of a car. He did not need a car. He and his family lived simply and well. But the customs of his tribe, reflected in the advertisements and the imperious voice of the neighbours, made it necessary for him to have a car. A car was a good thing to have. Other people had cars. Without a car he lacked something that contributed to the fullness of his life.

The only way in which he could get the money to buy a car was by caving in his best friend's skull with an iron bar, and then robbing him. The clumsy murder was quickly discovered, but the government psychiatrist declared J. to be subnormal. The death penalty was commuted to life imprisonment.

There was a time when a moron, if he moved at liberty at all, was known as such by his habits. It was then a simple matter to protect him from society and society from him. But this unfortunate man was not identifiable as a subnormal. Neither the work he could do, nor the amusements he enjoyed, nor the conventions of his behaviour were different from those of the people with whom he associated from day to day. A full measure of civilised behaviour is not expected from subnormals. They are sensitive to influence, unsteady in judgment and abrupt in action. Poor J. made the decision to commit murder because he moved freely among influences against which he should have been protected, and he translated decision into action because he moved freely and unnoticed among men who should have had protection against him. In one sense, and that a cynical one, the problem of *his* "rehabilitation" had been completely solved. The matter of fitting him back into

THE USE OF MORONS

society never arose. He had never been excluded in the first place.

That subnormals can live and work among normal people has tremendous implications. Considered as a social experiment in rehabilitation, it is all right so far as it goes; but that is a comparatively small matter. If the subnormal is known to be what he is, then this mutual protection can be given. If the subnormal is not known to be what he is, then man and society are the losers. The norm is itself moronical, and there is no social achievement in finding for the subnormal a place in a social scheme which is moronic. An occasional murder, robbery, and rape by the deficient at large cannot be met by polite tut-tutting or the remission of a death sentence. The real thing is how many people like J. are at large. And most important, where did they come from? The little poem with which I opened this book is not really funny at all. If those whom we know to be morons can move so freely among us, it is we normal, superbly intelligent, and totally integrated men-in-the-street who might be forced to reassess our own sanity. A moron? My God, perhaps I am.

A subnormal is usually identified by his inability to cope with common circumstances. If common circumstances fail to act as a sieve, sifting the backward from the bright, it does not only mean that the backward are going to move freely among us. Those who are bright are going to be tarnished. The normal are going to be the real sufferers. If the demands made on a man by society are no greater than those which can be satisfied by a moron, then the unwanted faculties of a normal

25

man will atrophy, and the next and near stage is the conversion, more accurately the subversion, of a normal man into a moron. Just how far is all this industrial progress making morons out of men? It is a question worth trying to answer.

II

MUSCLE AND MIND

THE ONLY way I could answer these questions was to go out and try working in order to have a closer look at the effect work had on men. Like most people who have suffered from the disadvantage of higher education, I knew very little about the world or the people in it. The best way of getting to know people is to work with them.

There was nothing patronising about this investigation. I had inherited from my original ancestor Adam an obligation to keep alive by working. At an early age I discovered that the things I wanted to do would barely keep me in pipe tobacco. I had two alternatives: to take a steady job for life—that is, to exchange freedom for security; or to take advantage of the post-war labour boom and become a job hobo. I tried both but preferred the latter. It helped me most in doing eventually the things I wanted to do, and it was as good a way as any other of earning enough on which to live. I have never had any job in which I was not, in some degree, dependent on the pay envelope. The jobs I had in England were always my sole means of livelihood. I mention that because unless the importance of the pay envelope in the worker's scheme of life is fully understood, no observation of working conditions is worth anything.

I began with a three-and-a-half-year term of security in the Australian government service. It was wartime and I had little choice. It was the only avowedly temporary job I have ever had, but it was the longest. It had its merits, but it killed any desire I might have had for security. After that, the longest term I spent in any full-time, permanent job was five months; the shortest, two-and-a-half days. Short working terms were of course preferable to long terms because the worst job becomes bearable after a sufficiently long time. This is not because the job gets better, but because the critical faculty of the worker gets worse. There were also the regular part-time jobs I had, some voluntary, some paid, and of which I always had some half-dozen or so going at once. They were part of what I considered my own work, and do not really belong to this saga of industrial vagrancy. Nevertheless I have drawn upon them for material.

My object was to find out external and obvious facts of working life which for many reasons could not be discovered by interview or visit. At the beginning I suppose I was not even sure what I was looking for. An explorer does not go into a wasteland to find anything in particular. He goes to find what is there, and to draw his conclusions from what he finds. I have always liked exploring; and it was curious that I always found more of God in the Australian bush than in the heart of civilisation.

What does one look for when exploring the wasteland of contemporary work? From wondering how many men like J. were at large, unnoticed and indistinguishable from their fellows, it was an easy step to wondering what the general effect of work was on man; how, that is, man reacted to his environment. That is what an anthropologist looks for when he studies the Esquimaux or the Tierra del Fuegans. It might just as well be what a sociologist looks for when he studies the modern man at his work.

The lowest form of human work is unskilled physical labour. An animal can pull or carry heavier loads than a human being, but the lowliest human being has a certain power of judgment in such matters as picking up, direction and setting down. Where loads are great and the necessity for decisions is small, the horse or the ox is more useful than the labourer. Where the work is in a confined area, where loads are lighter and more decisions have to be made by the carrier, the human labourer is more useful than the animal. For large-scale mass-movement of material, animals, and indeed men, have been replaced by machines: the grab, the conveyor, the chute, and the belt. There is an implacable certainty about machines, which sometimes has its disadvantages. The human labourer is still in demand, in spite of his load-carrying limitations; he is an elastic machine capable of varying his behaviour as contingencies require.

In the realm of human affairs, the larger the business the greater the general proportion of unskilled physical labourers. In the realm of human affairs, too, the "big" business is rapidly ousting the small business. Such businesses are important then for both reasons. I signed on the pay-roll of such a one, a paper mill employing about six hundred men. It was related to several similar plants and subsidiary companies, and the whole organisation was a big combine. The opinion of the shop steward, the trade union representative on the working staff, was that it was a "good" shop. His opinion was endorsed by all the men consulted. Worker-management relations were cordial. A central committee of workers, personnel and management staffs dealt with matters of common interest and contention. There were ample social facilities, personal amenities, and the organisation of the continuous shifts suited the private life of the workers. The personnel officer, a gruff young Scot, believed sincerely that none of the men was overworked. He had their welfare at heart in much the same manner as a farmer believes in conserving the energy of his horses. But he did not know how true his opinion was. The men were certainly not overworked. Their attitude to work was openly hostile. By common consent they had chopped about an hour a day from their forty-hour week. True, everybody sprang into life when a company official hove into sight, but work was systematically avoided when he disappeared again, and the finer points of how to avoid it without being found out were explained to newcomers. It was easy to hide in the rambling buildings of the plant, and one man's proudest boast was that he had survived a whole shift without once falling into the error of working. There were hidden recesses for poker and two-up schools, into which the newcomer was carefully introduced after a few days. Part of this initial schooling was the art of standing attentively alert by a machine while reading a comic paper. If an industrious newcomer was driven by sheer boredom with cards and comics to carry out his work, he was corrected with comments that soon became hostile. The first warning was a tolerant opinion that such diligence was "not necessary". If the conscientious beginner persisted with his folly, the tenor of the remarks became more antagonistic. The output of work was reduced literally to the limit of the foreman's watchfulness and the saturation point of absolute idleness.

The optimistic Scot had deliberately overstaffed the plant in order to make sure of average production with under-average effort. There was comparatively little work for each individual to do. The workers were all unskilled, and after only a couple of days I was able to take charge of one of the big ˙machines. Most of the work consisted in carrying loads of pulp or waste paper by hand or trolley; emptying these loads into beaters; feeding sheet pulp to beaters; sweeping and cleaning, shovelling, raking, or stacking. A handful of chemists darted out occasionally, in white coats, and darted back into hiding again with a torrent of friendly abuse behind them. A couple of crane-drivers worked high above the heads of everyone else and seemed to delight in swinging mighty bales of pulp as close to the heads of the men below as they could. But these were the only men with any semblance of skill.

The object of the mill, and this I believe to be a fundamental point which will be more fully discussed below, was the making of low-grade paper, chiefly for wrapping. I mention this because paper-making is an ancient craft, and the development of paper-making machinery might have been one of the noblest steps towards genuine progress that science has given to a suffering world. Paper-making machinery is enormously big and it has great beauty and dignity. Its essence is a system of rollers, over which the saturated pulp from the beaters is slowly poured until, by the sheer length of the journey (in one case, a hundred and fifty feet), the fibres are knitted together, and the wet slop at the feeding end is transformed into a giant swathe of delicate paper which flows off the other end onto a storage roller. We are so accustomed to the sight of paper in convenient sheets that there is something delightful about an unbroken sheet of paper ten feet wide and hundreds of yards long. There is something to marvel at in the sight of these slowly turning rollers, several feet in diameter, in a sequence as long as a running track, caressing the pulp into this long carpet of paper. That such machinery builds the paper by the delicacy of its touch instead of mangling it to shreds is a remarkable testament to how admirable machinery can be. But to see one such machine, gently moulding a pulp dyed pink into a mammoth roll of paper pinker still, and to know that all this human skill and knowledge was destined by the grace of big business to wrap chewing gum, was to make one feel sour. It is difficult to become fervent about work like that. I felt as I feel when I see circus elephants playing with coloured balls and wearing silly hats. A thing which has greatness and beauty and a capacity for doing even greater and more beautiful things when the hand of man guides it rightly should not be made to do less than its nature demands simply because someone is going to become rich by it.

The workers themselves, in this mill, were a rabble; they were not ignorant clods redeemed by the dignity of knowing their ultimate and infinitely more important destiny. They were loud-mouthed, dogmatic, and evil-tongued men who had apparently committed every sin in the calendar, and were proud to admit it over lunch without the omission of a detail.

I would never have believed it possible that the sexual life of man could be revealed with such vigour in such dispassionate activities as rabbiting, the races, football, or the comic papers. It was impossible to say that conversation ranged over these matters and sex too, for sex was the connecting stream of thought which gave meaning to all the others. Not one thing was allowed to pass without its sexual significance being demonstrated to the innocent. This erotic interpretation of life was accompanied by the appropriate rituals. There was a certain amount of flippant homosexuality. The organs were occasionally produced or displayed. It may comfort the fashionable ladies who insist upon having their parcels wrapped to know that the paper was freely impregnated with urine. Had Freud lived to see it, he would have been a happy man. Not even Havelock Ellis could have demanded fewer inhibitions.

The mental standard of the workers was, of course, low. So-called lack of inhibition is always accompanied by, indeed only made possible by, a stunting of the intellectual integrity of man. Reading matter—there was a lot of reading done—consisted of comic papers, pulp weeklies and dirty magazines, most of them scavenged greedily from the waste-paper bales which arrived daily for

33

repulping. The men had a curious inability to describe or explain. One of the surest tests of the cultural standards of any people is their ability to tell you where to go if you ask the way. A Roman policeman could tell me the exact whereabouts of a men's lavatory four blocks away though neither of us could speak the other's language. A worker at the mill could not tell me, in several hundred words of our common language, the whereabouts of the hot-water urn, though it was less than thirty feet away around a corner.

So far as unavoidable work was concerned, the general plan was to try and leave it to someone else. There was of course a flat taboo on doing anything which was officially the task of someone else, whatever the consequences or circumstances might be. This had some picturesque results. A beaterman by the name of Henry who became a mate of mine had a blockage in his beater ten minutes before the shift began. Blockages were frequent and the first remedy was to take the long pole kept nearby for the purpose and to try by force to ram the coagulated pulp through the submerged knives. If this did not work, the beater had to be stopped and emptied. A man got in and cleared the knives by hand. This operation took about five minutes. To be sure, enough ramming always produced a sufficient clearance to prevent the beater overflowing, but ramming became very tiring after a while. Henry put up with the blockage for the whole shift, indulged in the masochistic luxury of fury and frustration, and finally took the skin off his shin because he would not stop the machine and clear the blockage the proper way. That act of maintenance and repair was the official duty of a man named Joe, who had not been seen all day. Joe was hardly ever seen. Whenever my beater was blocked, I cleared it myself, as much for the pleasure of a break in the monotony as for any higher motive. But Henry took the view that if the illicitly-conceived and base-born Joe was going to desert his mates and play poker all day, he Henry was not going to do his job for him. Henry finished that shift in a state of exhaustion and self-righteousness. Joe, of course, was totally unaffected, and quite unsympathetic. His only comment was rich in wisdom: "Why didn't the silly barsted knock off and 'ave a smoke."

There was no law or rule involved and yet this kind of self-flagellation occurred again and again. Those who have studied human attempts to refine the principle of evil may find much to think about in such apparently trivial cases. Why indeed did he not knock off to have a smoke? Why do men do things which to others are obviously absurd? Anger, impatience, self-righteousness, are all the symptoms of a human being out of touch with reality. And being out of touch with reality is only a broad definition of insanity. Henry was not certifiably insane. Since, by his interest in politics and the reform of the banking system, he regarded himself as a man of some wisdom, he would no doubt be outraged by the accusation of imbecility. But certainly he was less sane than Joe.

This plant was a "good" plant. It was approved by all legal, civic, industrial, and union authorities as a fit and proper place for men to work. Why? Because there were hot showers, cafeterias, and other bodily comforts.

Everybody was contented in a bovine way; even Henry did not nurse his grievance for long; and although quarrelling, spiteful revenges, and querulous complaints were fairly continuous, the energy of the workers themselves was so sapped by the grazing-paddock atmosphere that it was easier to accept the patronising favours of their masters than to work up much enthusiasm over any other issue.

This vast workshop, making paper for chewing gum and for wrapping, was stamped with all the badges of excellence it could obtain. The mass-production of a low-grade article for an even lower-grade purpose was recognised by King and Parliament by the granting of a knighthood to the chairman of directors. A knight used to be a man who knelt in vigil before the Blessed Sacrament before risking his life in the defence of honour and virtue.

There was on the pay-roll a genial halfwit named George. George was not only the best worker in the mill, he was also the happiest. He was a big sprawling youth of twenty years of age, with the brawn of a giant and the mind of a child. He could truck more bales of pulp than any other man, for his body was too strong to be exhausted by that sort of work; and his mind was too weak to become restless through lack of mental activity. He whistled and sang in a growling tuneless voice; nobody ever had the slightest idea what he was singing; probably he did not either. If it had not been for the influence of his companions, George would have been a perfectly integrated worker. Conversation bored him but he loved company, and like all his kind, he had a child's vanity. He sniggered proudly when anyone took notice of him. It became a popular game to tell George dirty stories for the fun of hearing him re-tell them. It became fun to tell him to leave all his buttons undone. George enjoyed this because it made him the centre of attention. He became even more the centre of attention one day after a wag had told him something else to do. Nobody seemed to think that the brand of humour which caused the poor halfwit to expose himself in his desire for popularity was anything but funny. The foreman roared hell out of George and he retreated to the lonelier but happier life behind his trolley. He was inclined to distrust his workmates after that; his eye took on the same glint which may have come into Adam's eye after tasting the fruit of the Tree of Knowledge. It was curious to see what knowledge could do to one like George.

The mill provided security of employment if the most primitive idea of contract was observed. Short of open mutiny, or downright provocative behaviour, the management was not prepared to force an issue with a worker. Manpower was short and somehow the wheels could be kept turning with the low-grade manpower available. That was all the management cared for. To worry about the energy of individual workers might have caused trouble with the whole union, and the risk was not worth taking.

Security, easy work, no harsh discipline, an impersonal management, these things almost add up to a workers' paradise. The result was laziness, irresponsibility, viciousness and obscenity. Perhaps there was a cause and effect between the two. The halfwit George was happy, his mates were not. George was fully occupied because he was a halfwit and therefore did not need much to occupy him. His mates were never fully occupied even when they were busy. Their mental habits became like the feeding habits of a goat with too much freedom. A goat snaffles ravenously here and there, continually moving on restlessly, unable to concentrate on one thing effectively and heading always for the most obvious and the most easily obtainable. Thus, for the goatlike mind freely ranging over an area of mental wasteland, sport, comic papers, loud talk, and obscenity. The power to concentrate on things judged by the intellect to be good is another mark of sanity. Hence the ascetic ideal with its acute awareness of the danger of being attracted to lesser things by the louder and less reliable judgment of the senses. The goat has always been a symbol of the devil because of its voracious inability to concentrate. It is a symbol of chaos. When the mind becomes goatlike, it may be the devil or it may be diseased. The two are often connected.

Then I went into a co-operative woolstore and again moved things from one place to another. The woolstore employed an even simpler form of labour. The machinery and processes of the paper mill, though they had removed the human element from the making of paper, could still interest a human being. But there was no machinery like this in the woolstore. The warehouse received stocks of wool, held sales on the premises, and sent the wool off to the buyer. The task of the labourers was to move the wool bales from bay to bay, or from floor to floor. They never knew why particular bales had to be moved; they were told only how many, from where and where to.

This might have been a deathly monotonous job. The store consisted of a number of linked sheds, each three or four storeys high. Each bay was a vast bare space, until the bales were moved in. Then it became a maze of narrow passages and tunnels. The bales had to be moved according to their markings and for a distance of anything from twenty to two hundred yards. If five hundred bales are to be moved by five men, one at a time, a lot of steady plodding behind the laden barrow is necessary. The work was physically stimulating after one acquired the knack of handling a bale. Some skill was essential in this, not only to move the bales but to reduce the danger of injury while handling them. Between floors, elevators were used, and the mobile lifters were called in to build a high stack.

The work was seasonal, and few of the men knew each other personally. There were no amenities of any sort, no cups of tea, and only the most primitive of washrooms. The only rest periods were those between the ending of one move and the beginning of the next. The men worked mostly on their own and it was not a satisfactory job for learning much about them. They were a varied crew as seasonal workers always are, but although they were villainous, they had a certain stature which lifted them high above the men of the paper mill. Their language was obscene; it was raucous obscenity, not sniggering lewdity, and so far as one can make a legitimate distinction in such matters I prefer the former. Several

39

of them were seamen, temporarily ashore, and they were proud of their ability to move bales without the help of friend or trolley. There was no limit to the amount of strength that could be used, and some used more than others for the very clear reason that they liked to show how strong they were.

Childish? Perhaps more accurately childlike. They did not have much to be proud of but they had something; and that is the beginning of self-respect. The only machines were those which helped men, not replaced them. The result of the day's work could be seen at a glance. Although concealment was possible, although the policing of each individual was impossible, still there was no suggestion of loafing, and the work was done quickly and well.

There was no security in this job. Only a handful of men were on the permanent staff; the remainder were engaged for a period of either weeks or months. They could come back year by year but for at least six months they had to find something else. The work was plain labour without any reference to origins or ends, but strength was an asset and muscular co-ordination was essential. The moving of wool bales does not seem to be much of an art; but muscular co-ordination is. Weight-lifting, which many people wrongly think to be the most bovine of athletics, does not depend solely on brawn. It calls for the right use, at the exact second, of all muscles; there is a complicated decision to be made. The thrill of weight-lifting is that, failing this precise co-ordination of every part of the human body, the man finds himself in trouble with the weight. Muscular

co-ordination is only necessary when the weight exceeds
the normal lifting power of the particular limbs applied
to it; and an error of judgment when lifting in this
manner leads to torn muscles or a squashed body. Any
activity which demands the harmonious operation of
the body, each part in tune with each other part—
whether it be dancing, mountaineering, or load-lumping
—can call for exact decisions. Exact decisions are what
morons cannot make. The standard of education in the
woolstore was low but the standard of intelligence was
high. There was a certain sharpness about the men, a
quickness of movement, and with it a quickness of mind
that is often produced by a well-disciplined body. A
self-pitying shirker received no sympathy at all. He
found the work too hard, and since most of the men
liked showing how strong they were, they could not see
his point of view at all. There was something of the
exuberance of a football team about the gang.

There could not be much love of work in such a place,
but the work was done and the men were well paid for
it. Those in charge were seen at work themselves, and
if the manager had to move a bale he moved it himself;
and showed at the same time that he could. The manager
had a knack of making men work with him rather than
under him. He could do every one else's job slightly
better than they could.

There was no other way of doing this work, and it was
itself a work of integrity. The buying and selling of wool
is a legitimate act of commerce, and in order to carry it
out the wool has to be moved by man in certain ways.
It has to be moved by men who are strong enough to

do so, who can make a judgment in stacking, and can use their heads when a stack begins to wobble. These demands made on the men, and the nature of the work itself, were, I think, important.

The ten-hour night shift of the Victorian railways goods yard was spent in unloading a weird variety of goods from railway trucks. Cheese, farm machinery, crates of poultry, boxes of eggs, cans, bicycles, engines, vegetables, sheet metal, and an altogether indescribable collection of other goods were carried short distances, never exceeding twenty yards, and at a uniformly high speed. The labour used was casual, and was recruited week by week from a regular pick-up post. The pay was good. Once these goods were stacked on a platform according to a set pattern, it was the responsibility of someone else to move them. The work was not physically tiring, but the length of the shifts—five unbroken hours before a meal and four after—added to the monotony of the short movements, made it a very wearying night. There were no rest periods, except when walking from one emptied truck to the next full one. Most of the men were filling in a week or a fortnight between other plans and a few knew each other personally. There was a large number of foreigners. Language was no bar because directions were confined to indicating the object to be moved and the place to which it was to be moved. All this was done in a huge and very cold shed. The quiet of the night was broken only by the occasional hoot of a locomotive, and, in the shed itself, the pounding of feet and the scrape of the iron wheels of the barrows.

There was no conversation, only an occasional raised voice. Each man was preoccupied with his own job. No mental effort was necessary; the amount of physical effort was small. The work was constant and it was intolerably dull. The general conditions of work were bad: it was night, cold, dark, intense, and relentlessly monotonous. But it was done by the gangs with extraordinary efficiency. They moved quickly, handled the goods with care, and night after night the goods came through and were kept moving.

This was another job which could not be done by machinery. The human labour element was essential. And since the public transport of merchandise is a necessary economic activity, the work has integrity. But it needed no skill. It was labouring in the strictest sense of the word. Men had not been subordinated to the machine in a socially useless work; men retained some of their dignity because only men could do this work; but it called not even for the primitive skill of the woolstore labourer, and so it was more exhausting work. More exhausting, but it was not stupefying.

Labouring is not the simple thing it seems to be. It is still the most common of man's works, but it is never the same. The man who is hired to fetch and carry may be made into a man or a moron by what he is asked to do. Just how far it can make a man was shown by the standard of the employees of a fruit market store. Jammed in among a score of similar businesses in Melbourne's Victoria Fruit Market was a wholesale fruit business which employed me for several weeks. The market shop was only one of many branches and although about forty to fifty men were employed, they were a fluid group who moved among the other branches from day to day or week to week. The atmosphere was one of continual bustle and hurly-burly, of customers, of rival fruit-sellers, of loud voices and outdoor activity, of trucks, trolleys, barrows and loads.

The efficiency and morale of this shop were tremendous. No man knocked off before the day's work was done, and the day's work was so erratic that it might be any-thing from six to twelve hours. Work began as early as each man could get to it, and that meant fantastic hours by ordinary standards. The first man began at 4 a.m. and all the staff had arrived by 6.30 a.m. Knock-off time varied from 12 noon to 4 p.m. In the open air of the early morning, it was fresh and invigorating. The tasks consisted of loading and unloading vehicles of every size from Lister auto-trucks to five-ton semi-trailers; stacking, re-stacking, moving crates, packing crates, delivering, and for the élite of the store, bargaining, buying, and selling.

The boss was a fat self-made Jew who was neither liked nor respected by his men. He was ingratiatingly friendly to his staff and tried hard to be one of them but never quite succeeded. The fault was only in the limitations of his personality, for he was just and fair, and worked as hard as anyone. When he fussed and harried them, they answered back freely. He was certainly not feared nor was he even invariably obeyed. He accepted this insubordination because he knew that the work would be best done in this way.

Some of the best men I have worked with were in

this business. When I first applied for a job there, the young foreman told me it was just "dirty donkey work". Nobody ever describes his work to a prospective employee in those terms unless the job means something more to him than just a pay envelope. The language and conversation of the shop was clean and fresh, they were men of courtesy and intelligence, of physical strength, gentle manner, simplicity and resourcefulness. A desire for and need of order was the essence of their work. In a limited area, stacks had to be neat and accessible. Every man knew the origin and destination of everything he handled. They were proud of the fact that they worked hard, that they were doing a man's job.

Again, they could not be replaced by machinery in any way. What machines they had were completely subordinate to them. As a business it was an honest business. It was hot with the argument of haggling buyers and sellers but was certainly more honest than many smooth shops where inflated prices are immutably fixed by backroom boys. It was moreover a shop which—honestly—supplied food, thereby adding a necessity for its existence to its business integrity. I do not suppose any of the men employed consciously thought of these things at all. But men have a habit of accepting without question a right state of affairs, and they are capable of knowing intuitively a wrong state of affairs. This was a shop which called not so much for a skill—the work was nominally unskilled—as for intelligence and initiative. Each man, as a result, had added more work to himself. The trade unions would hate a shop like this: it had gone so far towards solving the problem of human peace by means and ends antagonistic to the whole union philosophy. These unskilled labourers had made their jobs more complicated because it came easier, they could do it better, by using more of themselves in it. They liked it better that way. They preferred to be hard-working men, rather than nursed working animals.

It is in places like department stores that the humble labourer assumes a more gentlemanly aspect. Department stores are noted for sham gentility, for obsequiousness and above all for vulgarity.

It was in a large London store that I made a foray into laborious gentility by becoming a porter. Porters are supposed to be rather higher in the social scale than labourers. But their work is the same. They may wear a collar and tie under their overalls, they may be called "Mr.", but all they do is carry parcels. Goods arrive in the receiving dock and have to be carried to the appropriate part of the store. They are sold, and if the customer wants them delivered, it is the porter who carries them to the despatch dock. I worked at all points along the line. The surrounding faces were different but the parcels were always the same.

Work in the reception dock was placid, for the men were old-timers who had been with the firm for years. They did their work and questioned neither its purpose nor the morality of their masters. They took their pay envelope as the fulfilment of a contract and talked without heat about politics, football, or films. The senior man was an imperturbable old character named Pop who warmed my heart by giving me an hour for morning

46

tea, ninety minutes for lunch, and another hour for afternoon tea. Since each of those intervals fitted in with slack periods in the dock, nobody was the loser by our leisure being applied to refreshment. The firm might have made a loyal supporter of me if they had not transferred me to the despatch dock as assistant to a man called Rabbit.

He was called Rabbit by way of satire. His own name lent itself to this nickname, but otherwise the only resemblance was his timidity. And since that timidity only expressed itself in the presence of someone higher in authority than himself and was replaced by a quite opposite disposition to authority in the presence of his own personal staff, the resemblance did not go far. Rabbit was near the retiring age, and had been with the firm for fifty years. His father had been there before him. In fifty years, Rabbit had risen two rungs of a long ladder and had just got his smoke-stained finger-tips onto the bottom hem of respectability. He was paid £1 a week more than I was, but the difference between our ranks was infinite. I wore flannels and an overall, he wore a black coat, striped baggy trousers, a frayed collar and a heavily stained waistcoat. He had a dripping moustache, and his first word of greeting to his newest flunkey was an order to take my hands out of my pockets.

He might have walked out of a novel by Dickens; he was one of those arresting people who are living testimonies to original sin and the lack of sanctifying grace. Rabbit was mean, spiteful and officious, a coward and a bully, and he sublimated his terror of authority by exerting what little he had himself over his staff. He

47

was guilty of unashamed acts of discrimination and his whole moral code was based on the ability of the other person to hit back. In a work of fiction, he would be regarded as a grotesque caricature. He was not, of course, a fully developed man. He was a product of circumstance, and certainly I could not detest him as much as I pitied him. It was impossible either to like or to dislike him, just as it is impossible to be emotionally aroused by an aggressive wasp. But he was impossible to work with, and that is why, in the fullness of time, I was fired.

I was totally dependent on the job at the time, but managed by the grace of God to get another in a few days. Whatever value Rabbit may have had, and as a man with a soul he had a lot to his God, he was unfit to have any authority or control over anybody. A man of no education, with a family to keep, driven by economic necessity to service in this firm, might have his life cruelly twisted by the stupid antics of this embittered old man. And only in such a place could such a man have such authority. He had the power to destroy the happiness of man, and, what is worse, he wanted to, because he hated mankind. A good man tied to him would become like him, just as Rabbit was probably the handiwork of some earlier nineteenth-century bully. Only in department stores have I found surviving the crouching attitude of servitude which was the triumph of the nineteenth century. The reason is because department stores can now only employ the weakest and most susceptible of men; and their masterpiece is the occasional Rabbit.

But he, though a prizewinner of his kind, was unique only in degree, not in kind. His superior, the goods manageress, was a middle-aged career woman with the manners of a headmistress. She was a very silly woman, because her intemperate and petty attitude towards her almost entirely male staff caused trouble to everyone including herself. I worked with a man named Bert who was a skilled fragile packer. Packing is the nearest thing that a department store offers to craft work, and Bert was as happy in his work as a terrier. Because of his drooping jaw and inane grin, many of his mates took Bert for a halfwit, but in fact he was a highly intelligent young man. Although he could not pronounce the names of any of the composers correctly, he was passionately fond of classical music and he knew their works well enough to whistle them all day long. Every day, he skilfully packed an average of twenty-four china sets, each item separately in straw-filled wooden cases. He was expert and conscientious and had never had a breakage reported against him.

It was near Christmas however and the flow of chinaware was coming faster than Bert could cope with it. He asked for assistance and an old man named Sam was transferred from another packing room to help him. Sam packed forty cases a day because Sam was an old hand who made a bee-line for the smallest lot every time, and he packed them like a tool-box. Bert went on selecting the biggest and most difficult lots because he enjoyed solving the problems they posed. The two of them just kept the line of goods under control, but the manageress was not satisfied. On one of her rounds she informed Sam that she was satisfied with him, but that Bert would have to increase his daily output to thirty cases. There was no special reason for wanting thirty, she only reduced to an exact figure what she really meant by the word "more". She left Bert near to tears.

The number of cases did not matter because they varied so much in size, and Bert knew that he was doing more and better work than Sam. There is a certain normal speed at which the good workman proceeds, between the pace of the reluctant worker and the pace of the impatient rusher. It varies from man to man because it represents the pace of efficient working and no two men are exactly alike. To a good workman, speed does not enter into it unless there is a special reason, and in Bert's case the Christmas rush had made him increase his speed as much as he considered compatible with efficiency. To tell him to do more or to work faster was to insult him; and in this particular case, it took away any respect the workman might have had for his senior. What she said proved her total innocence of the problems of a packer, and an innocent person cannot command things of which they are ignorant.

The manageress, as a woman, was not wholly blameworthy. What she knew about men came from the lessons learnt in a fashionable education, and what she knew about labour relations came from the "experts" who think labour really is a marketable commodity. This view of man, descending from the higher level of capitalism and theoretical economics, has been endorsed from below by the trade unions. In most cases it might be necessary to tell a workman not to be a loafer, because his unions have told him so emphatically that he ought to be a loafer. The unfortunate thing was that Bert was a normal

healthy young man who liked work. He was not pene-
trating enough to see the real reason why old Sam
earned praise for dodging work, earned praise from
both sides as well, while he was accused of loafing because
he liked work. Bert was the odd man out in this scheme
of things. Two people with a disjointed sense of reality
are more likely to gang up together against the one sane
man than one of them is to see the sane man's point of
view. The effect of course is to reduce the one sane man
to their level. If the good workman finds his work is
not satisfactory, then the invitation to him to lower his
standards, and therefore himself, is clear; it is not only
an invitation, it is an order. Bert nearly wept, not solely
because of the insult but also because subconsciously he
saw this command. And being normal, he did not want
to become subnormal.

The manageress was a problem not only to the labourers
but to others higher on the executive ladder. Some time
after I left, one of her assistants, an executive who had
been with the firm for eighteen years, turned in his
resignation. He could endure her no longer, he said
sadly. Perhaps he had somewhere else to go, but department stores are notorious for their cultivation of un-
employable types, both manual workers and white-collar
men. Once absorbed into this form of work, they become
of very little use to anyone else, and their lives depend
upon holding their jobs. It was hateful that people
like Rabbit and the manageress should have the power
of making so many people unhappy, and should use it
with such utter irresponsibility.

The porters in this firm were pathetically respectable.

Dominated by the bullying figures of their two masters, they remained nevertheless a tranquil gang of middle-aged family men who pursued their work with enough interest to get it done. None of them liked it, but the only complaint they made was against the obstruction and tedium of red tape, and the self-importance of minor executives. The instinct every man has for order helped them to keep a line of goods moving. Every porter's job boiled down to getting the goods away as soon as possible after they came in. They had to keep the stream flowing. If the goods moved out quicker than they came in, they had a rest. If not, it meant congestion and confusion and their energy was doubled to get the line under control again. Their language, behaviour and manners were above reproach; they were kind, thoughtful and temperate. In their own small way, they were useful men. They were useful to the old ladies who could not carry their parcels, and they were useful to the children whose Christmas toys had to arrive by a certain date securely labelled and packed against the tragedy of breakage.

Outside their world was the ruthless world of the store itself, and it was this ignoble work of buying and selling, of obsequious discipline and impersonal hypocrisy that left its mark upon the executives. The staff bulletin published the names of those who had made "errors", standing them as it were in a corner for making a wrong charge or entering a sale in the wrong ledger. The grandiloquent titles bestowed upon little men, the deadly serious nature of staff organisation, procedures and formulas, gave to these men a great sense of importance.

This sense of importance, deriving not from what they did but from what they called themselves, expressed itself in their relations with each other. It was like a nightmare fairy-tale. Above the bottom layer where the porters worked usefully and enjoyed their own pleasant company, the whole atmosphere was thick with childish make-believe and dramatics.

There was not much security for the porters. So little in fact that I was fired for the only time in my life. The turnover in junior staff was extensive in spite of inducements offered to all ranks to stay. The wages were barely enough for a single man but there was a system of family allowances which lifted the wage of a family man to a reasonable level. This of course made it economically impossible for family men to leave. Workers like me could walk out with a snort or be fired with a jeer. But a family man with neither skill nor trade, in middle age, cannot afford to lose a job like that. The wonder is that those workmen retained as much self-respect and decency of character as they did, for they were a fine team of men worthy of better masters than they had. Above all they were never childish; and that is the only word that could be applied to the make-believe of the rest of the store.

It was during my term with this firm that I was also a lift-driver. For one who has outside interests, a liking for private reflection and any desire for solitude, the piloting of a goods-lift has many pleasant features. The driver is imprisoned from the sight and conversation of man. He is called to duty by his buzzer, and in a lift

53

where there is no outside indication of his position, he can take his time about answering the buzzer. The beauty of my lift was that nobody, not even I, knew exactly where it was. I could anchor between floors and read away happily to myself. The imperious summons of the buzzer reflected only the impatience of the waiting load somewhere, and if it was not answered immediately, a lying impression of being a very busy lift-driver was given without any necessity for verbal explanations. The only labour involved was the pressing of a button, the turning of a handle and the opening of a door. This lift was used only at intervals, and in the delicious solitude of the lift shaft, I devoured the books secreted in my overalls. But only rarely could lift-driving be so idyllic. Its pleasantness depended entirely on having plenty of other things to do. The driver of a public lift, continually on call, exposed in his cage like a monkey to the critical scrutiny of passengers who begrudged him a moment of delay, ascending and descending and repeating like an endless juke-box the chant of "Pyjamas, boys' clothing, men's underwear, and accounts orrrrfice", would have a hellish life. Lift-driving was fine for a journalist with a notebook in his pocket, but what it would be like for a man with nothing of his own choosing in his head I do not like to think.

Any job where the mind is completely free can be not only tolerable but refreshing. But if the intellect is to be stimulated by it, this stimulation must be consciously sought. Uncomplicated manual labour is only beneficial to people aware of and with a use for their intellect. If the intellect is ignored, it becomes an open tip for every kind of mental garbage which others have thrown away, thrown off, or wish for their own reasons to pass on. The intellect cannot remain empty. It can either choose its contents or be filled without making its own selection. There is no limit to the rubbish with which it can be filled if its owner refuses to make any selection.

Now although it was apparent that a worker's attitude to work was not necessarily improved by security, that it often deteriorated in the presence of great security; although it was clear too that the integral usefulness of the job was reflected with startling clarity in the attitude of the men towards it, the most surprising thing to me was my own personal reaction. I knew theoretically that men can and will work well as labourers, whatever their intelligence. I did not know until I did it how well men can work if certain conditions, quite outside the sphere of labour conditions and touching only the most profound part of man, are fulfilled.

In at least half of the various processes and assignments spread over these jobs, I was perfectly happy and might have been prepared to remain there for life. That I did not do so was only because there were other things I wanted to do more. There was nothing repellent in the jobs themselves. That I felt so contented was not, I hope, because the smallness of the demands made upon me satisfied my desire to loaf. It was because each of those jobs gave me the chance of doing more with my whole self. The demands made by the job were confined to certain parts of me. The satisfaction of those demands did not trespass on other parts of me left free, and since I could do what I liked with them, there was an opportunity for a very real satisfaction of the whole man. How relevant so much "industrial welfare" is to the provision of true contentment at work was shown by one picturesque phase of my working life. While at the paper mill, the halfwit George and I were often assigned to shovel straw. This was the filthiest job in the mill. As George and I were the only two men in the mill who enjoyed this job, we were given the assignment as often as it came along. We crouched, stripped to the waist, underneath a giant spherical boiler, forty feet in diameter. In this boiler, the straw was "cooked". When cooked, this sodden mass of foul-smelling straw was dropped from the boiler between us, and as it came slowly out of the boiler, piling at our feet, we forked it onto a conveyor belt. We stood knee deep in this awful stuff, unable to stand upright because of the boiler overhead. In the hot atmosphere, we sweated until we glistened. This was the kind of work that had all the thrill of a mountain climb in it, and I loved every moment of it. So did George. In that reeking atmosphere, every bone and sinew of our bodies strained—struggling, crouching, forking, and perspiring— dopey George and I found a common interest and friendship in the type of work nobody else wanted to do. Why was this?

Both our bodies were used to the fullest and most exhilarating extent. That in itself is a wonderfully satisfying thing. True physical exhaustion, derived from a united action of the whole body, is a condition of great contentment. George had nothing to think about, and nothing to think with. So he was totally immersed in his work. I had plenty to think about and could, because my

56

thinking parts were not only unimpeded, but actively stimulated by the intense activity of my body. The greatest thoughts a thinker ever has are the thoughts which coast uninterruptedly, gently, and smoothly through a mind that is undistracted by the demands of a body because the body is either totally occupied or exhausted into submission.

This kind of completely manual work is fit only for morons or for students. Whether or not manual work makes a man or a moron depends not only on the exact nature of the work, but also on the type of man who takes it up.

III

CRAFT AND CLERKS

WORK IS classified by the jargon of modern in-
dustrialists as unskilled, semi-skilled, and skilled.
Since the first two are practically identical, I
do not make this distinction. The difference between
unskilled labour and semi-skilled is only the difference
between a human horse and a more adaptable kind of
primate who can be taught a few elementary motions
in a matter of hours or days. Labourers, for some reason,
are often classed as semi-skilled. But "semi-skilled"
describes more accurately the state I was in when I went
into the carpenter's shop. I took with me not only my
brawn, but a small quantity of knowledge picked up
untidily from my own workshop. I could not guarantee
to hit a nail straight but I knew which end of the nail
to hit. I knew that a dovetail was not only to be found
in a dovecote but should be found where two boards
met at right angles. The world has seen more notable
carpenters than I, including the most notable of all men.
It may have seen worse; I do not know. But at all events,
a carpenter's labourer is not really a labourer. He is
not supposed to be as good as St. Joseph, but he is supposed to know more than a trucker of parcels.

I was employed as a carpenter's labourer in a small
workshop where there were fewer than twenty men, most

of whom were skilled tradesmen, or apprentices. No unskilled men, as such, were employed. When goods had to be carried, material stacked, or work done which called for labour, everyone lent a hand from the boss downward. The shop made signs and hoardings for petrol companies. It called itself an advertising company but was in fact a construction company on a small scale. The work included carpentry, skilled and rough; riveting and metalwork, rough painting and skilled signwriting.

Each man was given and left to an allotted task, and in each task skill was necessary. The result of this was absorbing work. There was little opportunity for loafing; none of the men had any inclination for it; nor did the absence of the boss for the day make any difference. There was co-operation, a sense of partnership, of responsibility and dignity. The quality of work was frequently referred to. Never too serious, and often in the form of badinage, there was still a real appreciation of good workmanship. Indeed, there was so much that was excellent about this little workshop that the one jarring note merits discussion.

An apprentice and I did a heavy job of riveting for about ninety minutes. When we finished, we were tired, and we sat down on a timber stack to smoke. The boss appeared suddenly at the office door. He took no notice of us, but the apprentice jumped to his feet, stubbed out his cigarette and signalled me urgently to resume work. On one other occasion, a new employee was dismissed— "laid off", as they say—without notice or explanation after only a few days. He had been "tried out" and found lacking, but he never knew what it was he lacked.

Nor did he know that he had been on trial. He was a little bitter about it, and there was some muttered sympathy from his workmates, for in the few days he had been there he had made good friends.

The boss was a diehard Tory, and no suggestion of worker-management equality entered his mind. His son had worked in the shop before going into the office, but there were two men in the shop who had worked much longer than the boss's son, and they were still, in the fullest sense of the word, employees. By policy, it was a non-union shop, and the boss told me once that I could not find "a more contented lot of workers anywhere".

Both he and his son based their industrial policy on the premise that they were, in their own estimation, a jolly good pair to work for; he said so in so many words. And the staff was contented, it is true. They were happy about their work, but, like the staff of the fruit market store, they had a certain quiet contempt for both the boss and his spoilt son. They were making things, the boss was only making money; and if the boss made money from their making things, they would not change places with him, nor mind very much so long as he left them alone. So far, so good; but the crux of their relationship was something that can only be called servitude. They did not own their work. They owned only their skill, and this they had sold outright to the boss. The boss was using their skill for the primary purpose of making, not things of beauty, but profits. He was a business-man, employing artists for his own business-like ends. The boss was not a better craftsman than any of his men.

He was simply a better business-man, that is, a better maker of profits. He had the skill, if such it could be called, to husband other men's skill to his personal gain. And they lived in some fear of him, for no matter how hard they worked, or how long, or how well, their life as artists could be ended by a whim of the boss. That is why the apprentice jumped back to work when the boss appeared. That is why there was some sullen comment when the new man was turned out.

The hours were good, the pay was good, the boss was fair and just in a crude way, and the work was good. Even a petrol-hoarding is something to be made; it is an ordered harmony of timber, metal and paint welded together into a whole. Even if the purpose of it is to disfigure the landscape by its invitation to swell the overflowing purse of Mr. John D. Rockefeller, at least by itself it is a conjunction of skill and material, and the man who made it is generally a happy man. Carpentry, of course, was the profession of Christ. Since there was meaning to every detail of His life, I have often wondered why He chose to be a carpenter. That He should choose to be a craft worker is obvious, for reasons I discuss more fully below. But I have never known why He chose to be a carpenter in particular, nor do I know why woodworking is actually the most beautiful of the crafts. The reason for the one is probably the reason for the other. It may be that of all God's material gifts to man, wood is the most richly amenable to use by man. There is practically nothing that cannot be made from wood; and the types of wood, the methods of treating and finishing it are the most richly various.

What excitement there was then when this instinct of man to take raw material and to hew from it a form commanded by his intellect was turned from the making of a petrol-hoarding to the building of a chapel in the bush. Whatever happens to the community of young men who fled like the Benedictines from the world of Melbourne and Sydney to the Whitlands bush in order to give their whole worship to God without distraction, I shall always look at the chapel we built from the logs of the forest and say, "The roof is mine". They did not pay me for doing it, not in money that is, but they recompensed me for my labours in a way that can never ever be explained to a person whose mind bears the smallest smudge of economics. They kept me, sang to me, dragged me from a deep warm bed on frosty mornings to the chanting of Prime and the singing of Mass; and in return for an altogether revolutionary effect upon my soul, I laid the beams for the shingles on the chapel roof. If you look closely at this roof, you will find it slightly out of alignment. The hand of man, especially this man, is not always true even when putting a roof over God, but perhaps it is then that his hand shakes most.

Perhaps it is not fair to regard this as a job to be compared with other jobs. But it was "work". If I had not done the roof, one of the "monks" would have had to desert the fields to do it, and deserting the fields meant fewer rations. So for several weeks I clung to the high arch of the roof, with a rope slung around me in case I slipped, in crisp air under a warm autumn sun, with a majestic view of the wild deep hills before me. I hammered and sawed and sang whoopingly. Periodically we knocked off to unleash some psalms of the Divine Office to the glory of God; we paused, that is, in our work to contemplate God; and then we scurried back to add creation upon creation, to build to the glory of God. The whole chapel was built from the raw wood of the forest, from the massive logs of the walls to the delicate cabinet-work of the tabernacle. It is the most beautiful chapel in Australia.

I worked on this chapel with a boy of massive intelligence who had a fiendish stammer and appalling nerves. He had fled from a breakdown in the city to recover his sanity. With the aid of a hammer and nails, and a psalm in the evening, he did—much to the perplexity of his psychiatrist, who had suggested some mechanical remedy. I wished the psychiatrist could have come and worked with us and he might have recovered too.

The essence of carpentry is the direction of the hands by the mind, and the preoccupation of both body and mind attendant upon this is one of the most integrating of human experiences. An almost equally fascinating modern craft is electricity; and an extraordinary effect of work on man was demonstrated not so much by the effect of this job on me as the effect it alone could have had on the men I worked with. The place was a theatre. The hours were long and, because it was a theatre, included all those hours normally given to leisure. The pay was good but the work was erratic, irregular and unpredictable. Each man had a personal set of daily assignments, but occasionally all teamed up together for urgent jobs. My own job was first to sweep and clean the workshop. Since it was frequently used for drinking parties after the performance each night, the diligence of a surgeon was needed to restore order first thing in the morning. Then I checked the waterpots. The dimmers belonging to the theatre, as distinct from extra dimmers hired for plays which needed them, were old-fashioned waterpots. The electrician on the switchboard pulled his dimmer lever. This pulled a cable leading to the basement underneath and on the end of this cable was a plunger in a cylinder of water. If the plunger made contact with the bottom of the pot, the connection was complete and the light was full. If the plunger was lifted, the current had to flow through a variable quantity of water before it made the contact, and the light was proportionately less: the more water, the less light above. If the plunger was lifted just above the level of the water, the current failed to pass at all and the light went out. The water evaporated quickly and the level had to be maintained with some precision each day. I refilled the pots, measured them with a dipstick, and then checked the light on stage to see that the rate of dimming was even and gradual. Another job was to repair the radio set. This radio set was an iron box, appropriately painted and disguised. When the heroine turned on the switch, a torch battery inside lit the dial; another wire, loosely connected, led to a signal light above the music turn-tables, and when the technician received this signal, he supplied the music which the audience thought came from the "radio". Then the leading man stormed onto the scene in a raging fury, swore loudly and hurled the radio through the glass door. Each morning I collected this radio and repaired it. The amount of damage varied, but it was my job, at any cost, to have that radio rewired, with a fresh bulb and dial if necessary, and back in position on stage before the performance that night. During the performance, I operated a travelling lime-light which followed the heroine like a faithful hound throughout the performance. Then there were the irregular jobs: repairing a fuse in the box-office, installing an Exit light over a new door, scrambling out across the chandelier, and gathering in lampshades from the circle balconies, like small boys after seagulls' eggs. There was plenty of variety.

The gang was a bunch of raucous Cockneys whose conversation and interests seldom deviated from a low level. The standard of their anecdotes and allusions was hair-raising. They drank, swore, blasphemed, argued ferociously among themselves, and made offers equally wicked either by way of threat or persuasion. At times they committed the most shocking mistakes in their work. A theatre, especially the stage, is more the object of public scrutiny than most places where people work. A leading lady depends for her success on nothing so much as on light. Not even her talent can survive in the dark. Dominating the electricians was their gargantuan Chief, Bill Jones, a living reproduction of the original John Falstaff. He was a great fat man, middle-aged, monstrous in some ways, naïve in others. His most memorable act was to mount the switchboard one night, swaying unsteadily and breathing alcoholic fumes over everyone, and to collapse like a vast sausage across a row of dimmer levers. This caused a play of lights and colours across the stage which neither the stage crew nor the leading lady have ever forgotten.

Bill was the kind of man who could bellow the order "Quiet" with such sincerity backstage that he could be heard in the back stalls over the orchestra. He was also a craftsman, and so were his staff. In nearly every case the work was done with the precision of artists because the staff never thought of doing it any other way. In the few cases where there was failure, it was due solely to the intrusion of a too great human element; that is, failure was never due to the direct neglect of work, but only to the intrusion of some other distracting element which prevented the work's being properly done. Even on the night when he collapsed on the dimmers, Bill had been determined to carry out his routine inspection, though he knew he could hardly stand up straight. When he did fall, it was while on duty. It was just bad luck that he fell across the levers.

I was the only man in the shop approximating to a Christian. Bill, in his own aggressive words, was an "affiest". I was the only one who did not regard sin with undisguised exuberance, but I do not think that our friendship was impaired. It is possible for there to be two types of man, both of whom tell the same stories, make the same suggestions, and apparently have the same base desires. Yet it is easy to see the man who is in touch with reality and the man who is not. The animal contentment of one marks him as a man who has found a level of satisfaction below his true level as a man; the other shows the symptoms of a struggle which it is in the nature of man to endure continually. Bill Jones suffered from much unhappiness. He found partial relief in drink, noise and enthusiasm for the little pleasures of life which included both his girls and his goldfish. The recurring bouts of depression, anger and sentiment told of a man whose very contact with reality kept him in a state of war. Because he lacked full understanding, he had to suffer a lot. It may be coincidental, but I do not think so, that such men can almost be typed from the work they do. Bill Jones was, to all appearances, an utter scoundrel, and yet there was a deep well of goodness in him which lifted him high above many men of outward moral observance who would have been disgusted by him. He may have been exceptional in degree, for he was a great personality. But that same well of goodness existed in all those craftsmen who worked with him. Of course they were corrupt, but we all are. But their work protected them from that abyss of corruption into which such tragically great numbers of the working world fall. The goodness in them was able to flower; and there is a lot of goodness in man, if we give it half a chance.

The world of so-called civilisation regards manual work as very lowly, and handcraft as a "trade". The most desirable vocations for the sons of suburbia are the "white-collar" jobs, and the least skilled of these—but still socially more acceptable than the base trade followed by Jesus—is that of a salesman.

I experimented with three kinds of salesmanship: in a big store employing several hundred on the sales staff; in a small shop employing only two; and as a commercial traveller.

Salesmanship is a career which makes a strong appeal to the ingratiating, bustling type of man who wants to feel important. It is a palatable substitute for creative work. Unfortunately the price paid for being a good salesman is high. It is a new career, a direct and bastard offspring of the mass-production economy. The mass-production economy took the word "craft" out of the language and gave us instead the word "crafty". A good salesman has to be crafty. The better salesman he tries to be, the worse a man he becomes. A pity, but true, for many good men have had to become salesmen and few have succeeded in perfecting both sides of their character. The mass-production economy is based upon the production of quantity. So great are its overheads and running costs as a result that it cannot relax for a second. Sales must then be forced. The selling of a thing becomes an object in itself, regardless of whether the thing to be sold has any purpose. True salesmanship was defined by one enterprising American as "making a person who does not want it, buy something that is no use for its supposed purpose, when he cannot afford it anyway." Perhaps not many carry the theory of this to an actual practice. But most would if they could. This represents a fair ideal of the expert salesman.

I have already talked about department stores, and all that need be added is a note on the utter servility required of the salesman. He is expected to be "well dressed", that is, conforming to an artificial pattern. True courtesy is squeezed out by an abasing servility, not only to one's employers but also to their employers, the customers. This grovelling attitude of the customer-being-in-the-right, to be an object of constant appeasement and placation, originated in the nineteenth century. It was introduced from the bazaars of the East where it is a calculated strategem aimed at the vanity of white travellers. Two Egyptians bargaining among themselves use a quite different technique from that which both use when a European comes along to buy something. I have an Egyptian friend who throws department stores into confusion by trying to bargain with an obsequious salesman every time he goes in to buy a handkerchief. It is a curious reversal of the norm in his case, for this servility is deeply rooted in the big stores of the English-speaking world. The most outrageous insults from customers must be passively accepted. The person is not used simply as a horse, as in the worst cases of physical labour. The salesman is employed because of his human faculties. These divinely given faculties are used by others, cast aside when not required, turned this way or that at the whim of the customer or store manager, and above all taken away from the person to whom they rightly belong. He is not permitted to use them at all. One of the most insulting things a customer can do to a salesman or salesgirl is to ignore them. To stand behind a counter, required to do nothing more than display goods to a buyer who resolutely refuses to acknowledge your existence as anything beyond a pair of hands which lift articles from a drawer, is a trial of the spirit second to none. It may produce a saint, but it is not just to impose on so many men, women and girls the conditions which may make a saint from one in a thousand.

The thing called "discipline" is carried too often to

the extent of tyranny. In a London store, a notable feature of the weekly staff journal was the column "Partner's Errors". In this column appeared such reports as:

"Making an incorrect charge: Mrs. N. N. CH Dept.
"Charging goods to wrong customer: Mrs. N. A. CH Dept.
"Failure to notify customer of delay: Mrs. E. F. COS Dept."

This firm had a good reputation for worker-management relations, but nobody seemed to think this kind of behaviour anything unusual for adults.

There was a rule in another store that an employee was not permitted to "do nothing". When business was slack, he must find something else to do, such as tidying up, or walking about on patrol, or even "looking alert". He was as fully bought and as fully misused as any man could be. His intellect was used for displaying, cajoling, or even lying; his body was dressed up and put to attention. Competitive selling, the equipment for which was almost only fast smooth talk, was the only outlet for his enthusiasm for life. He was expected to connive at such practices as giving false information to customers. I know. I have done it. I have taken off a 3s. price-ticket, put on a 9s. price-ticket, and marked the price down to 5s. for a "sale" of "colossal reductions". When I protested my masters were indignant—not that I should threaten to reveal such practices, but that I should dare to think such practices dishonest. My career as a salesman, they hinted, was in jeopardy because *I* could not be trusted. At such times the only thing in jeopardy was my own sanity.

A salesman is a merchant: that is a go-between for maker and buyer. He has a useful function to perform as agent. He can be an adviser; he can go out of his way to satisfy the exact needs of the customer by his more detailed knowledge of the market, he can be something of guide and friend to the customer. In the little shops where I sometimes buy specialised equipment for camping and travelling, the salesman is the expert. If he recommends the more expensive article, I know his opinion is valuable because sometimes he will recommend the cheaper. He knows the subject better than I do, and I go to him in humility for the sake of the professional service I can get from him. But the department store salesman picks up only a few scraps of knowledge about goods which are simply given to him to sell, and his recommendations are a patter of clichés designed to relieve his own boredom rather than to be of value to the customer.

To be a good man and a good salesman is not easy, but I knew one who succeeded. He worked in a big store from no choice of his own, but once there and determined to make something of his life, he rationalised his repellent occupation to the service of helping people to be clothed. At first, his position in the store was most precarious. If some rubbish was left on the counters, he told the customers that it was rubbish. If he could not supply what they wanted, but knew a store which could, he told them that too. The management was outraged.

They allowed him to stay only under the closest super-vision. At the end of his first year, his sales record was equal to that of the other salesmen. At the end of his second year it was substantially better. At the time of writing he has the biggest sales-sheet in the store. The management, though they now treasure him, cannot understand how he does it. But the reason is clear. He can be trusted and he has built up a personal following. He never deviated from his policy, and that policy became known to customers, and through them to their friends, and he has been sought out by those who need an honest helper with their buying. He is still an embarrassment to the firm which employs him because he so resolutely refuses to connive at any of its underhand practices. I hope that he may have partly persuaded them that in the long run underhand practices are not even good business. At all events he, who was the world's worst salesman by all the canons of sales theory, actually sells more goods, and helps more people, and thereby builds up more good will which in turn is converted into more customers, than any of the experts. He does this not because he is an expert himself but because he is a Christian. He did so however only by at first running a big risk of being fired for incompetency.

What he did is extremely difficult to get away with in a big store. Policy and rules are rigid and impersonal. In the small toyshop where I worked later, the climate was totally different. The boss was a ridiculous character who had worked himself, not without some courage, from a street-corner market stall to being the owner of a high-class toyshop. He had the inclinations of a saint, but the mentality of a spiv. So he was always in a state of tremendous indecision. He could cheat a customer without turning a hair, but later he would begin to worry, especially if his staff of two looked at him with raised eyebrows. For days afterwards his conscience would torture him. He was always working out the grossest plans to bolster up his sales, and then trying to justify the plans by appealing to the highest and most scholarly forms of ethics. He was a very funny man to work for.

Nevertheless, in such a shop the employee can achieve two things. He can acquire such an intimate knowledge of the business that a relationship of servitude cannot exist unless the employee himself wants it to exist. If it does so exist in a small business, it points to something really wrong with the employee. Secondly, the relations between employer and employee when both are intimately in touch with each other depend entirely on the men concerned. It can only be a personal relationship, and as such, it is the personalities of the two men which govern their relationship to each other. Which is as it should be.

An employee can make something of a job like this. If the boss is a lunatic, of course, working conditions may be difficult or impossible, but even so he is easier to endure than a similar lunatic in the position of foreman or under-manager in a big organisation. The little man Rabbit could have me fired by the department store without ever mentioning a word to me. Being a coward he could do it behind the scenes. When my toyshop boss tried to fire me, I told him not to be absurd. If the master is an impersonal monster, the employee can only become an impersonal microcosm. If the employer is a tangible person, at the very worst the employee can never cease being a person himself. This however can only apply to establishments where there is a staff of less than a dozen. In general, and there may be notable exceptions, impersonality tends to enter working relationships when the staff approaches fifteen or twenty and becomes almost certain when the staff goes over fifty. One exception was the fruit market store where the personal element was healthy with a staff of about fifty. But the conditions and work were also exceptional.

A commercial traveller is, of course, by the nature of his work an individual. That does not prevent him from being an unscrupulous brigand. There would be no image of the vacuum-cleaner salesman with his foot planted in the doorway, leering at a besieged housewife, if enough travellers had not behaved in this way to create the legend. If he is a sales shark roaming the seas of suburbia in hungry search of commissions, then there is no limit to his nuisance value. But even then he remains an individual and his position is more akin to that of a bandit than of a moron. He needs all his skill and all his personality to be a competent bandit. He may be cunning, but he can never be a fool. On the other hand he can be a highly skilled merchant whom customers are glad to see because he brings them newer and more useful tools and equipment for living.

For a few glorious weeks I was the roaming vendor of a princely apple-peeling device. At first the project seemed an unashamed racket; even the thought of such a thing as an apple-peeler still sends my friends into fits of laughter. The idea of hawking such an object around the streets of London is hardly compatible with human dignity, and had I not been so impoverished at the time I would never have done it. But nobody could laugh when he saw the light that came into the eye of a kitchen skivvy working in the basement of a big hospital when she had seen the demonstration. Nobody could feel useless after the open-mouthed joy on the faces of chefs and underlings when they saw what the wonderful machine did. And the machine sold, as a result. After a while one walked into hospital kitchens feeling like an angel of light. It was like distributing largesse to the multitude.

Between the big store and the small shop, there existed the difference of being a human personality or not. And the same difference existed between the Federal civil servant during wartime, engaged for a specialised job of administration, and the permanent State civil servant who is the most clerkish of clerks. The miserable clerk cannot help seeing the contrast between what he is supposed to be and what he actually does. I was a clerk for a short time in the Penal Department. My task lay in transferring to personal record sheets, in the neatest of handwriting, the names of citizens incarcerated in the local gaol. That was all, and no more. This job was carried out in an atmosphere of ties and jackets, of polite surnames, of awe and fear. I came to love passionately those whose spirit of primitive independence had brought their names to the sheets I copied so industriously day after day. I felt an intense desire to walk out of the door and let my name be placed on that roll of honour which passed across all our desks each day—the drunk and disorderly, the intemperate and the rebellious, the Magdalens and the spirited revolutionaries who refused to conform to the design for respectability which the statutes of society had forced upon man. These mutinous people whose names I meekly copied were the forerunners of divine order, for they knew what a precious thing human personality is. We in the department presumed from the heights of our judgment-stools to condemn them—entering their names in the column marked "Offender", and listing their joyous conduct under the column headed "Crime". There were of course some who overdid it. Some were too exuberant. There were even some who were morally culpable. Some should not have done what they did. But they were only about five per cent of the total.

I knew many men with whom I had been at school who had enlisted in the permanent public service or some similar administrative post for the sake of the security and prestige it offered; and also because they thought, as one would naturally think, that the public service was what it called itself. If an idea creates an organisation to carry it out, the organisation can quickly kill the idea, and the idealists of yesterday are too often the obstructionists of today. Why, I do not know, unless the reason is to be found in the curiously wayward nature of man. It is always the way.

During the war I served temporarily as a clerk in one of the permanent departments. My work consisted of receiving certain incoming correspondence (which was in triplicate) and re-routing it to its three separate destinies. For that I had to be highly educated. The fact that I had flunked a University degree by being too interested in other "cultural" activities nearly cost me the job, but they considered that I must know something by virtue of the sheer length of time I had spent around the University. I was asked to be presentably dressed, and had to put on my coat and straighten my tie when summoned by the director. A man cannot stay in a job like that for too long and stay normal. Whatever beneficial effects secular higher education might have, even they would soon be rasped away by the sheer indignity of allowing a mind that was keen for action to be dragged along behind the plodding coat-tails of someone older whose illusions had been shattered a long time before and who before his fortieth year was bitter and sour. This playing with paper is too big a part of the public servant's life and too big a part of the life of almost every office worker. Private administration, when it becomes big and organised, is invariably more cluttered with "red tape" than even the worst government department. It is a vice belonging to offices. Office administration has become a childish make-believe with its records and references, cross references, double checks and systems. The apostles certainly did not have a filing-cabinet between them. And I doubt if any one person who ever really made a mark on the world had one either. It is a pretty game but it has little relation to what is actually done.

The sense of fury and frustration which comes from battering one's head against an immobile system or arguing with a foolish old senior clerk must be distinguished from the fury without frustration that comes

77

from a failure to achieve a good end by meeting the duplicity or roguery of one's fellow workmen. In the Federal wartime department, each officer was left very much to himself. He had a job to do and he did it. I could sit on the desk of the Assistant Director in my shirt-sleeves and argue with him as man to man, and usually the one of us who had the better argument won the day. There was a total absence of all the ritual with which an organisation that at heart knows its own uselessness tries to cover itself in order that it will seem respectably efficient. In an office which works, everybody is too busy to bother much about this ritual. The work done stands on its own merits.

Nevertheless we did have trouble getting certain things done. We were concerned with re-arranging civilian supplies in order to soften the effect of the war-time economy on those who suffered most, and these were of course the poor, the weak, the solitary and the aged. The department employed a large number of so-called expert "business-men". While the ostensible duty of these experts was to bring to the government machine the "practical experience" of big business, their actual achievement was to protect as far as they could the rights of the large, powerful combines they represented. This made our task of protecting the weak very difficult. But although on many occasions the small coterie with whom I worked were driven to extremes of fury by the advice and recommendation of these magnates, although they blocked our path with ruthless regularity, there was no real frustration. Frustration is a painful clash of the intellect with something it cannot grasp or comprehend. A stupid old clerk or a senseless piece of routine can frustrate painfully. A plain rogue does not. One has an intellectual appreciation of his motives and methods, and although he can make you very angry, he does not leave you biting your nails, tearfully wondering who is going potty, you or the boss. When sanity meets insanity, the sane may be doubtful. When the enemy is undisguised evil, at least sanity can be salvaged.

A mistake commonly made by people studying the nature of employment is the assumption that "monotonous" work is not pleasant, and "varied" work is. If by monotony is meant the repetition of the same elements in an unchanging sequence, then the most monotonous of all work is acting. Night after night, it might be argued, the worker is required to go through an identical pattern of bodily movement, of words, and of vocal inflections. Nobody however will seriously say that acting is monotonous. The question is, why is it not?

A post-office letter-sorter sits in front of a number of pigeon-holes and passes an eight-hour shift by sorting letters into their respective holes. This is an essential public utility. It cannot be done by machine. It demands some intelligence, and a first-class memory is a great asset. In the post-office where I worked, the sorters were left alone without restrictive supervision, and perhaps the prestige of a public service job that lived up to its name added some degree of dignity to the job. There was no sense of servitude. There were frequent rest periods because the work was enervating. Never to my

79

knowledge were these rest periods abused by the men or criticised by their superiors. The idea that the mail must go through was accepted universally and at peak periods this meant overtime. It was taken for granted. The standard of the work, the morale of the postmen, the relationship with their superiors and the climate of the sorting office left nothing to be desired. These things are not coincidences.

One man on the permanent staff had the title of permanent relieving postman. He was a privileged individual whose status was based on his knowledge of the names and addresses of every person in every street, not simply of one round, as in the case of an ordinary postman; nor of one district, as in the case of an old postman; but of six postal districts. He also knew a good deal of their intimate personal history; but that was unofficial. If people knew how much postmen knew about their private lives they would tip them more at Christmas time. Whether the P.R.P. found his job monotonously unpleasant I cannot say; but he was certainly one of the most intelligent, quick-witted, and happiest men I have known.

The most completely unpleasant job I had was one process at the paper mill. We stood on the edge of a slow-moving channel of pulp and at intervals of about ten seconds we threw in a sheet of pressed pulp. I do not know why. It seemed like flavouring a pudding with some special spice. The physical movement was the same as flicking a large sheet of strawboard across the floor. The mental effort was limited to an approximate judgment of ten seconds, or the corresponding space in the flowing channel. Both body and mind were occupied with the least possible activity. There was no release for any of the unused faculties, and since they represented about 95 per cent of the whole man, it was the nearest ever to doing nothing. Since doing absolutely nothing is torture, I felt as though I would burst after about fifteen minutes. Running a very close second to this job in unpleasantness was the position of clerk in the penal department. My body did nothing except perch precariously on a high stool. But at least I could get up and walk to ease my stiffened limbs. I could not do this while feeding the pressed pulp as we were subordinate to the machine. At the desk my hand wrote and my intellect registered a column of names. I did not stand either for long. There was too much of me chained up and howling for action.

The unpleasantness of a job has nothing to do with whether it is repetitive or not. It depends solely on how many of the parts of man are being used and how well they are being used. Acting is monotonous in the literal sense of the word; but few occupations use the whole man so intensely, and that is precisely the reason why it fascinates so many people. If a part only of a man is being used, the salvation of his sanity depends on what he himself does with the unwanted parts. (But if ostensibly the whole man is bought by the employer, and only a part is used, or parts are wrongly used, and the worker himself is denied right use of his own parts, then his sanity, in the sense of the fullness of his personality, is in danger.) Either the unwanted parts atrophy for sheer lack of use, or they are mutilated by misuse, and he ceases to be a whole man. It is because men have far more parts than they think, because they are far more complex creatures than is generally known, that most of the trouble occurs. And how little is known about the extraordinary size of man's personality, how little is known about the depth and variety of his delicate mechanisms, is shown only too tragically by the choice men themselves make when they seek what they believe to be good for them. Too many seek with great energy and enthusiasm the things which are going to have the worst possible effect upon them.

IV

AMBITIONS AWRY

I WOULD LIKE to have worked in every known type of job, but that was not possible. There are over five thousand occupations listed in the census report of the Australian Bureau of Statistics. This number represents only how workers of all grades, trades, and degrees of self-assessment have described themselves at the crucial moment when they filled in the census form. The report is unscientific to the extent that a street-corner salesman might describe himself as a "lecturer" as one whom I know quite well does—he claims to lecture on the merits of bootlaces; or a University professor may modestly class himself as a teacher. The report does however give a useful picture. Like the telephone book, the list is informative and makes entertaining reading.

Some time after it was published, I was called upon to talk to a group of undergraduates on careers. The word "career" is a bad one, as it suggests an energetic young person racing towards a goal of material aggrandisement. I changed the title of the talk to "Available Work for Budding B.A.s", much to the annoyance of the undergraduates. They felt that while a career was something worth having, "work" was another matter.

The students belonged to the Arts Faculty of the University of Melbourne. "Arts" has nothing to do with the arts as such, and Arts students, especially the young males, always have a slinking feeling that they are quite useless. The faculty includes all the liberal studies, the humanities, and the abstract sciences. It is the only faculty at Melbourne University which gives a university, as distinct from a technical college, education. Arts students go down into the big bad world with nothing more secure than the certificate of a good education. They have no automatic right to carve up bodies or estates, to build bridges or bombs. Their diploma does not tell them what they have to do for a living, so they have to make that decision for themselves. Since I had never even graduated in Arts, and had spent the best years of my life pursuing culture and the humanities with such zeal that I had neither career nor money of my own, they felt I was well qualified to advise them on this occasion. I confined my talk mainly to reading out the list of five thousand occupations and inviting them to choose the one that made the most appeal.

There were fifty students in the circle. The majority had a hazy intention of becoming teachers, librarians, civil servants, or of going "into an office somewhere". Some thought nebulously of a wide field called "radio". Some, even more rarified, felt called to "business". Nearly all were most concerned not with the kind of job they would get, but whether they would get a job at all. It had not occurred to them that they, as responsible creatures carved in the likeness of God, should be the choosers of their path in life. The choice was to be left in the hands of circumstance and the University Appointments Office.

Some of course knew quite clearly what they wanted to "be". They wanted to "be" writers or artists or famous actors and actresses or something equally exciting. But the boy who wanted to "be" a great architect had no interest in mathematics and was sadly disillusioned when told that the artistic method behind the construction of a great cathedral was mainly multiplication. And when told the present writer's experiences in the high-class world of literature, those who aspired to be writers merely decided that Brennan was not really a writer at all but simply a shiftless scribbler who was more concerned with making money than with art. Which was of course true.

The people who want to "be" something usually have a disjointed notion of what it is. The little lady who thinks of cool hands and feverish foreheads, who dashes off to become a nurse, finds her faith shaken when she does little more than clean the false teeth of querulous old men. Some professions are glamourised by pulp fiction, others are underwritten by snob standards of value. To "be" a surgeon is now socially excellent even though it may involve nothing more than untangling the overworked digestive organs of the rich and lazy. To "be" a surgeon in the days when a doctor was either a herbalist or an apothecary was to be a man merely useful without being in the least ornamental. Both then and now, the only really important thing is whether the aspirant wants to cure people. The sculptors who worked on the medieval cathedrals might be perplexed both by

the work and exotic status in society of Mr. Henry Moore.
And certainly the possibility of their son's being Lord
Abbot of a monastery would hardly move the parents
of today to such desperate measures as those taken by
the Count and Countess of Aquin to save their son
Thomas from the indignity of being a mere University
lecturer. The boiler-maker is a useful and skilful man
today. But in spite of all the people who relish his central
heating, hot-water services, Turkish baths and fast
smooth trains, not to mention all the people who make
fortunes in factories from his careful application of
steam power to their workshops, the status of his profession has declined in the eyes of a world which aspires to
"better" things for its sons. It is of course more than a
difference between "being" and "doing", for these
belong to each other. The popular notion of "being"
something really means "seeming" something. *Videre*
quam esse. Being a doctor means doing the work of a
doctor. To seem a doctor is much less energetic, and
can be a very enjoyable form of daydream. People
who have to decide what work they or their children
or pupils will do ought to make this distinction between
"seeming" and "being" more clear. Being requires
doing; seeming requires nothing, and amounts to
nothing.

University students ought to be able to take care of
themselves, however. Most cannot, but they are better
able to than that much larger group known cryptically
as the "working class". I met fifty intelligent members
of the Young Christian Workers' movement some time
later, and fired some questions at them. They were boys

86

between the ages of fourteen and eighteen, all of them
apprentices, all of them above average personality, and
all responsible officers of the Young Christian Workers.
Their attitude to work was uniform. Not one of the
fifty deviated from the fixed belief that his job was pleasant
enough, but that he would not be doing it if he were
financially independent of it; that he, the apprentice, was
the fool of the family, and could never advance to the
dignity of a white-collar job, but had perforce to learn
to work with his hands; that their job was "interesting"
was the best thing they could say about it.

I read to them an extract from one of Mr. C. E.
Montague's delightful essays.

The passing away of the greater part of that happy
excitement from so many modes of modern manufacture has been a real fall of Man. It has gone some way
to making work what it is said to have been to Adam
after his misfortune, a thing to be·got through and
borne with because you cannot go on living with it
upon other terms. . . . The thing has gone so far today
that at any trade union meeting, you would not expect
to hear a word implying the work its members do is
anything but a mere cause of weariness made endurable
only by pay.[1]

The Young Christian Workers did not fully understand
what Mr. Montague was talking about. Work was work,
a job was a job, a thing you did to get a pay envelope,
to keep alive with. The issue was as simple as that.

[1] From *The Right Place*.

No other concept of work had ever entered their minds.

The headmaster of one of Melbourne's largest technical colleges reported, when asked, that one of the really serious problems of youth-training was the refusal of so many parents to encourage a positive attitude towards manual or craft work. [He who is called the "clever" boy is kept at secondary school pursuing academic courses, and his logical end is a "white-collar" job. The boys who cannot make the grade, the dumb oxen of suburbia's families, are cast off into the wilderness of a trade, a handcraft, or of manual work.]

The Young Christian Workers, training for trades, accepted this indictment of themselves. Their status as apprentices they attributed solely to their having "no brains". They admitted it with jovial frankness and clearly believed the lie to be true.

The lie is a monster: a three-headed one, at that. A white-collar job is in no way superior to manual work, and I hope to prove that in the vast majority of cases it is less worthy of human attention than any other kind of job. Nor are "brains" necessary for the great majority of white-collar jobs. The stupidest people I have ever met have all been office workers, and some of them have been executives. But "brains" are necessary for craft work, or for trades.

The question arises, what is a white-collar job. It is a vague concept, but the term is so commonly used by the world that some attempt must be made to state its nature. There were five occupational groups classified by the Australian Bureau of Statistics. The groups, together with the numbers employed in them at the time of the 1933 census, were as follows:

(a) Professional and administration   256,462
(b) Domestic and personal service   242,378
(c) Transport and communication   223,893
(d) Trade, commerce, finance   451,172
(e) Industrial and manufacturing   934,691
(f) Rural   588,531

The much-coveted white-collar jobs are those of groups (a) and (d). A certain percentage of white-collar jobs are to be found in all the other groups; but the essence of a white-collar job is that it be administrative and/or financial. Of its nature it cannot be productive. A man who produces or makes something cannot be a white-collar worker as we understand the curious phrase. The white-collar, sometimes termed the cuff-and-collar man, uses a desk for a work-bench, pen, ink, and paper for his tools of trade, and gives no productive service to the community. I regret that I cannot think of a more complimentary definition, but it has taken me two years to clarify in my own mind exactly what this vague class or occupation is, and this is the best I can do.

He has of course a certain place in society. Economic life turns on an axis between making and using, between production and consumption. In primitive communities, the consumer produces what he needs. As society becomes more complex, the producer and consumer drift apart, and a third function appears, that of the

distributor. The distributive factor in society, sometimes more graphically called the lubricant, includes
of course the well-known "middleman". There is
nothing ethically wrong with this kind of work. The
middleman occupies the same role as messenger boy,
or lackey; he produces nothing by himself but he is kept
by society because of the small service he renders by
keeping the books or running the messages.

The middleman has a quite useful and necessary task,
provided two conditions are fulfilled: first, that there should
not be too many of his kind hanging around the workshop door waiting for the people who are producing
something to give him some work to do; secondly, that
he should not get any inflated idea of his own importance.
Neither of these rules applies today. The middleman,
disguised under the concepts of "trade", "finance" and
the like, is actually the most influential member of
society. He is drawing to himself most of the wealth
of society, and he is attracting an extraordinary number
of recruits to his ranks.

Look at these figures for Australia:

Production personnel (e) and (f) 1,523,222
Distribution (c) and (d)   675,065
Services (a) and (b)   498,840

It is impossible to separate "Services" from the office
of the middleman. Domestic and professional services
as such are simply more valid examples of the middleman, while the traders, the merchants, the transport
population are the middlemen confined to the actual

money-making life of the community. Furthermore, the "production" figures include all those engaged in the "administrative" side of production. What the other administrators are, God alone knows. The professional and domestic services include vast armies of lawyers, accountants, consultants, advisors, experts, hotel and catering personnel. While a certain number are undoubtedly of great importance to the community, there can be no doubt that the employment of so many unproductive people in these categories is evidence of a lopsided social structure. These figures indicate almost equal numbers of producers and non-producers. The margin between them is so small that it does not matter. A bouncing young country like Australia always absorbs the most progressive ideas. That it already has one cuff-and-collar man to every one-and-a-bit who actually contributes to the wealth of the nation is a glowing comment on contemporary standards of value.

Nor is it at all clear on what premise the white-collar job exercises such a fascination for those who contemplate their life work. It is certainly an intense preoccupation with "seeming" rather than with "being". So intense is this that I have met an extraordinary number of people who claim to "be" one thing, while actually they "do" something else. To be one thing, and to be doing something unrelated to it, is very difficult if not impossible. Being precedes doing and doing is contingent upon being. The integrity of a workman suffers seriously if he tries to separate the two from each other. A doctor I know is an uninterested workman so far as his profession is concerned, although no doubt he enjoys the large income it brings him. His private life is entirely taken up with exquisite cabinet-making. His woodwork is not only superior to that of most professional carpenters but certainly *pro rata* to his skill as a doctor. I do not know whether he would make more money at carpentry than at medicine; probably not, but the money-making side of any work is, or should be, the least important side of it. Certainly he prefers to "be" a doctor, and not a very good doctor either, rather than to "be" an artist at woodwork. To be a doctor is of course much better socially than to be a carpenter, regardless of whether one is a bad doctor or a good carpenter. Yet what he does—does, that is, with the greatest effect—is to shape wood. And therefore he *is* a carpenter, in a much fuller sense than he is a doctor; for he is most fully himself when he is acting as a carpenter. A worse case was a self-described actress who never obtained any acting work because she was no good as an actress. She had had some training but she had absolutely no talent. She had no interest in acting as such; she saw a stage only as something on which her illuminated figure could move before the concentrated gaze of a thousand pairs of eyes. She earned a living like thousands of other girls, either by typing letters or washing dishes. She never abandoned her claim to be an actress; she joined the relevant clubs and unions, and if anyone said she was not an actress, she screamed and stamped her foot. In fact she was simply a snob. She wanted to seem something other than what she was, something which she thought sounded better. This kind of silliness is very common.

The reason for these curious conventions is rooted in the complicated psyche of man. So much for the attitude of the would-be employee. The attitude of the would-be employer is not much more helpful.

At the present time the greatest demand for labour is for low-wage unskilled labour. This includes youth labour, and often includes the misuse of apprentices. Modern business began with the employment of babies in coal mines, and continued along these lines until forbidden by law. Youth employment has been tightly regulated, but the need for training young workers in skilled trades has left a certain number of loopholes for the exploitation of youth labour. Apart from these abuses, there is a tremendous demand for legally-permitted youth labour. It is still tragically true that many young girls go out on their fourteenth birthday, or whichever birthday it is on which they are allowed to leave school, to work in a factory or cannery. On their twenty-first birthday they are dismissed because they have then to be paid adult wages. The father of a very close friend of mine in Melbourne had a thirty-roomed mansion in one of the wealthiest parts of the city. He had a swimming pool and an electrically lit tennis-court, all of which he had acquired from a medium-sized clothing factory which carried a permanent notice outside inviting fourteen-year-old girls to join his staff.

The demand for youth labour is now greater than ever. During the slump years 1931–5, there was a widespread collapse in the birthrate. Birth-control was enormously popular, and the number of youths growing to working age today is ominously low. The shortage has reached its lowest point in 1952, and the normal rate, left behind in 1947, will not be reached again until 1955–6. God alone knows how much wealth and beauty, love and holiness was lost to the world in those terrible years of desperate struggle to survive. I suppose many of those who denied life to their children were afraid the children might starve. It is a pity they could not have foreseen the great demand for workers today, just when those children would have been looking for work to begin their careers.

The post-war boom created a labour shortage in most countries; in Australia, a year ago, there were a quarter-million declared vacancies in a total population of eight million. A prosperous picture, one might think. Unfortunately the employers, with a complete lack of responsibility, were dragging in both old and young into jobs which offered them nothing as individuals, but which could and did offer superficial amenities that made it very difficult for the young to resist temptation. Young people have been conditioned for so long to the wrong idea of work that the mere existence of so many jobs available for youth, at such enticing rates of pay and sugared with such splendid "conditions of work", makes it look very like the promised millennium.

Youth will learn of course but then it will no longer be youthful. I culled a number of wage rates from the jobs available for young people in Melbourne in 1950. The most promising offer for an energetic young man with the promise of a share in the business was a "nightman's offsider" at £10 weekly to start. For one who could endure this nocturnal collection of human excrement, this might have offered a future. Like the dustman, the job had a high social utility and the lowest possible status. But the wage was fantastically high. An unskilled labourer in a tyre factory (£8 15s.), and a foundry labourer (£8 5s.), were offered more than a qualified cook (£8 2s. 6d.); and a government sanatorium cook, presumably a more skilful man than either, was offered only £7 2s. 6d. As a carpenter's labourer, with no opportunity to learn the trade, I received £9 16s. The work could be done by any child with a liking for tools, but what child conditioned by our standards of value would take on a six-years' apprenticeship at virtually no wages at all when he could walk into such a lucrative post as this? A skilled builder's labourer, and an unskilled builder's labourer, received £8 17s. 6d. and £8 7s. 6d. respectively, both slightly more than was offered to graduate scientists for junior research posts.

Unskilled labour is commanding fabulous wages and the supply cannot cope with the demand. The last figures I obtained from the Commonwealth Employment Service showed 5,144 vacancies for quite unskilled labour, 12,150 vacancies for "semi-skilled" labour so-called (which I insist is, humanly speaking, unskilled labour) and 7,967 vacancies for skilled labour. The demand for "juvenile manual workers" is for semi-skilled and unskilled boys, and one of them, the "process worker", the lowest form of factory repetition work, is the most in demand.

The further figures I give below are taken from one country at one point of time: Australia, November 1949.

They are from the monthly returns given to the Commonwealth Employment Service. They can therefore only indicate a tendency, but the tendency itself is revealing. The actual labour demand, classified into detail, was this:

Carpenters	classed as skilled	839	vacancies
Fitters	,, ,, ,,	751	,,
Electrical and power maintenance	,, ,, unskilled	627	,,
Railway construction maintenance	,, ,, ,,	602	,,
Process worker	,, ,, semi-skilled	532	,,

(This was at adult rates of pay: an additional 494 at juvenile rates were also required; and to call this "semi-skilled" was nonsense.)

Engineers' labourer	classed as semi-skilled	514	vacancies
Sawmill worker	,, ,, ,,	511	,,
Labourer (unclassified)	,, ,, unskilled	506	,,
Motor mechanic	,, ,, skilled	500	,,

It might be recalled in passing that "process worker", which is classed as semi-skilled, and for which the greatest overall demand for both adults and juniors existed, was the job at which morons had been found generally superior to normal people.

The total demand for males distributed over all types of employment was this:

Rural and fishing	472 adults	98 juniors
Professional	1,340 ,,	19 ,,
(This included 1,201 teachers)		
Administrative	846 ,,	1,054 ,,
Skilled manual	6,715 ,,	1,252 ,,
Semi-skilled manual	9,008 ,,	3,142 ,,
Unskilled manual	4,584 ,,	560 ,,
Protective services	374 ,,	—
Other services	356 ,,	11 ,,

St. Thomas Aquinas classed agriculture as the noblest form of work. It is a pity that "rural and fishing" vacancies for young men were so few. I do not know what "professional" means in this context, but it is obvious what "administrative" means: clerks, messengers, small boys in their first felt hats. The demand for youthful manual workers I have again subdivided below; only the principal subdivisions are given.

Process worker	semi-skilled	494
Fitters	skilled	298
Knitting operative	semi-skilled	153
Railway maintenance	unskilled	140
Boot factory-hand	semi-skilled	132
Storeman	,,	116
Mill-hand	,,	116

None of these, except the fitters, remotely resembles a craft. Both the jobs of process workers and knitting operatives have proved admirable forms of employment for morons. To class a storeman as semi-skilled is another example of the abuse of the word. I have worked as a storeman alongside a genial imbecile only just released from an institution, and he was much more efficient than I was.

The chances, then, of the average young man's finding real work are very small. If he is very poor, he is denied education and finds no difficulty in settling down to life as an unskilled labourer. His choice of that vocation is rendered more likely by the enormous demand made by employers for such as he. He may be regarded as a human horse, and if so he will soon come to regard himself as a human horse. If he has "talent" of any sort, his logical end is an "office", or, if his parents can afford it, a "profession". The one prospect liked neither by boy nor parent is a craft, commonly called a trade. The boy prefers unskilled work and easy money. The parents want him to "get on" or "do well" in a white-collar job. A trade means further education, little status, and the sealing of the individual within the confines of a caste. Neither boys nor parents are impressed by the opportunity of becoming an artist, and the temptation of independence is offset by the insecurity which independence necessarily involves.

If one could only inform the minds of the young men of what they were missing by this silly attitude to work, how much more happiness could be given to the world. Take the matter of independence and security, for example. In the winter of 1949 there was a firewood shortage in Victoria. The constant unrest on the coal-fields increased the demand for firewood, and although prices were controlled and supplies rationed, the black market flourished. A timberman with a three-ton load could dump the lot in long lengths at a factory and get £8 a ton for it. If he cut it into foot or two-foot lengths for the domestic market, he never got more than £4 a ton; and of course there was much more work in cutting it into the shorter lengths. The houses of people who could not afford central heating, electric fires, or black-market wood went cold while the furnaces of industry crackled on wood. My family needed wood as much as anyone, so I went out and got some. The Forests Commission gave me a firewood lease over a small area of the Broadford hills, forty miles north of Melbourne, at a royalty of 1s. a ton. I drove out in my old truck, armed with axe and bucksaw. The fuel for the return journey cost me roughly 15s. I could have charged a price for the labour, but the timber was mine, I was an independent axeman, and it was absurd anyway to charge a price for spending days in the bush, stripped to the waist, and having the time of my life cutting and stacking timber. Wood-cutting should be a compulsory sport in all schools. It uses every muscle of the body, combines a need for strength, agility and footwork which makes it a cross between ballet and boxing, and the satisfaction of bringing down a forty-foot tree to within a few inches of the place you intended it to fall has to be experienced to be believed. I brought down a ton each day in six-foot lengths, spent about one day in three hand-sawing it into short lengths, and delivered it to my family and friends. I had far more orders than I could cope with, and was able to sell at £4 a ton. I cleared as much profit as a wage-earning wood-cutter would have received, and I was my own boss. I worked when I felt like it, began each day and ended it exactly when I pleased, and did not work at all if I felt lazy. Some days in the forest I took only half-an-hour for lunch, but then I could knock off any time and brew a cup of tea if I felt that a cup of tea was a good thing at any particular moment. One day I went to sleep after lunch and dozed in the sun for three hours. It was a hot day and work was not a good prospect that day.

I was able to live well on this although I was doing it by the most uneconomical methods imaginable. Had I been able to scratch up enough capital to buy a 3-ton or 5-ton truck, and to switch from hand-sawing to power-sawing, I could have increased my output five or six times without extra effort. I could have organised it better than I did. Firewood must be stacked properly and left to dry. I brought down a ton the first day and stacked it at home. It was not much more than half-a-ton the following day. I had brought down a lot of water with me. The wood should be stacked and left to drain on the site, and the longer it is left the better. The good firewood man stacks for the following year. All this could be done with planning, by careful purchase of the right tools and equipment. It was a gold mine of a business and a superb life. The physical effect on me was perhaps the most notable feature of it. I was producing a play at the time, in the evenings, and I heard that the cast was horrified by the change in their producer's character. After a day in the bush, a run home in the evening, a wonderful hot bath and change of clothes, I went out to rehearsal, as one player said, "like a rampaging bull". The effect on the intellectual or imaginative life of days spent swinging an axe in the bush is another thing that has to be experienced to be even faintly comprehended.

The danger with the firewood business was this: orders were flowing in far more rapidly than I could cope with them, and there was a terrible temptation to switch across to money-making. That means hiring labour; the boss sitting at home in his office growing fat and irascible with all the paper-work; the employees out cutting the timber and not enjoying it as much as I did because they would be working to hours, for a wage. Nobody would have been better off, because eventually the demand would have slumped and I would have had to sack the men or go into some other business: probably ice, like all the regular wood-and-ice merchants. All of which of course would have been crazy, because that was not why I went in for firewood cutting. I did not go in for firewood cutting to make money. I went in for it because we needed firewood. I found out I enjoyed it and could help my friends. I kept my other sources of income going at the same time, and when the firewood business closed down I was just as well pleased because some other demand had arisen that had to be satisfied. At no stage had I created an "industry" which was likely to take charge of me. I kept myself in charge of it.

Both the students and apprentices mentioned earlier were looking for the wrong quality in their work. Their attitude was identical, in that neither saw work as anything more than an unpleasant means towards the mediocre end of a pay envelope. They did not see work yielding anything more than a pay envelope. They did not ask more of it. Both saw it as a drudgery. The only important difference was that the students thought they had "brains", the apprentices thought they had "no brains". The students thought that any work which required "brains" would be "interesting", and many a young graduate has been appalled to find out that this is not necessarily so: that work with "brains" can be more deadly dull than any other form of work. The apprentices, accepting their condemnation to the brainless trades with calm philosophy, were agreeably surprised to find that their work *was* "interesting".

When I was abortively studying law at Melbourne University, there was with me a young man named David G. David was a pillar of solidity, respectability and rectitude. He did all the right things in the right way, including passing his examinations. He graduated, served in the war, married, and settled down in a firm of well-known solicitors. By twenty-six, David was as completely "successful" as any young man could be. I did none of the things he did and was regarded both by my family and friends as a shiftless hobo. What they thought does not matter. What David thought does matter.

Years after we parted as students, I straggled out of the bush east of Mansfield after one of my periodic forays into the wilderness. I was bearded and filthy and I entered the dining-room of the Delatite Hotel with some misgivings. But I was hungry, dinner was already on, and the bath could wait. There was David.

His unexpected presence in that dining-room seemed to me a reproof. He was as clean and well-tailored as ever; the only concession he made to the country-town was a suit of wonderful tweeds. You could not live the life I led, and endure the constant indictment of family and friends, without feeling at times that they might be right. It was one opinion against the opinion of the civilised world. Looking at David, it seemed that it was time I took example from him, and let myself slide as gracefully as I could into comfortable security. Certainly my aunts would be pleased, and I supposed that it must have its compensations for so many people to want it. Very few seemed to like the way I lived. David spoke first. He asked me had I finished my law studies. I told him the awful truth. "Lucky man," he said. "I wish I had failed like you."

He told me how he had been transferred to the Mansfield branch of the firm, how he loathed this picturesque outback town of dusty streets and cattlemen, because, as he said, "There was nothing to do" except play golf on Sundays. True, there was first-class trout-fishing, swimming, the best riding country in Victoria, horses, cattle, mustering, barbecues, and pubs which never shut. But David had not been brought up to these things. I felt like quoting to him the then popular American song:

THE MAKING OF A MORON

When they've got two weeks' vacation
they hurry to vacation ground,
they swim and they fish but that's
what I do all year round.

David was not the only one. Of all the students who
studied law with me, and then went out into the practice
of law, I have not yet met one who was anything but
resigned in a disgruntled fashion to a lifetime of tedium.
They were clerks and they knew it. Superficially it was
more complicated, but that did not alter its nature. After
the first flush of professional glory had passed away, they
saw themselves and their job at their real value. And
they knew too that the more a clerical job is wrapped
up in the colour packing of professionalism, the more
enslaving it becomes. It has been one of those coincidences that befall man that on two auspicious occasions
I was reported in the daily press as having taken
part in what was described as a "drunken brawl". On
neither occasion was I actually brawling; I was simply
shouting encouragement from the outskirts and was
therefore in a good position to be interviewed. Neither
was I drunk. But that would not have altered my fate
had I been in a position which required "keeping up".
In so many jobs which so many seek because they do
offer what they think to be respectability, these two
occasions might have been the end of their careers.
Fortunately my career, being non-existent, escaped un-
scathed from the scandals. But there you have it. Of
all the words which we have twisted out of recognition,
"respectability" is the most mutilated. It applies now

to men who, more than anything else, lack the respect of their fellow-men. A "respectable" man is a man beyond reproach, not only the reproach of good men but the reproach of all men, a man so submerged in the common mass that he cannot be criticised because he cannot be distinguished.

Nor is it only those who seek this form of "respectability" who suffer from the dissatisfactions of inadequacy. The awareness of inadequacy is nowhere more acute than among those who try to escape reality by being desperately unconventional. No one who has seen at close quarters the "emancipated" behaviour of students, "bohemians", or misguided intellectuals, can doubt the frightful tangle such people create about themselves. The worst language, morally speaking, I have ever heard was not from wharf-labourers or bullock-drivers, but from senior women students at Melbourne University. When the intellectual or the undergraduate searches for truth by ignoring or denying God, there is a mental contradiction akin to trying to square a triangle. If a thinker believes that he has succeeded, then he has twisted something out of shape, and what he twists is usually his own intellect. Such reconciliations are the mark of a special type of moron, a glossy type, with an impressive front, a depraved idea of man and a tendency towards a good deal of social beastliness. With such a man, logic of argument and the common standards of judgment have simply to be abandoned. There was a cultivated young lady of high aesthetic standards who vowed that music was essential to her life, that this was no mere figure of speech but the literal truth of what she meant: she could not survive without a weekly symphony concert. There was another young man who in a fit of pique tried to burn down one of the University buildings, because the staff therein had annoyed him. And there was a round of parties, in which festive relaxation took the form of nocturnal carousing spiced with various natural and unnatural vices. Please do not think that the manual labourers are the only unhappy men in our midst.

Nor is it simply unhappiness. You cannot tell a man who is well-fed, well-housed, and carefully nurtured by his wife that his happiness would be greater if he were more like a human being and less like a prize hog. The lowliest moron will always deny his affliction, since no man can imagine intellectual delights beyond those of his own powers. The more sensitive the faculties applied to a work, the more damaging to the individual if those faculties are not used properly. The labourer may turn into a clod by the misuse of his mental faculties as a whole, but a professional man can turn into something far worse—worse for being more subtle—if for example his moral sense is twisted out of shape by his work. When an advertising man tries to find a more persuasive line in ingratiation, the chances are that he will stimulate his already unruly imagination to a point damaging to his integrity as a man. When a lawyer concentrates on winning a case even to the exclusion of justice, he damages his moral sense, and therefore himself as well. A doctor who looks for a fat fee from a rich patient might prostitute his science in order to get it, and if he does he prostitutes himself as a scientist. Prostitution is always bad for character and it is not restricted to ladies. It is much more common among men. The sales promotion expert, who takes all the wonderful reservoir of creative power and organising ability of man and squeezes them into the narrow opportunities offered by a job like selling toothpaste is mutilating himself out of recognition.

A friend of mine, Tony C., reported that when he came out of the army, he was offered a post with a razor-blade organisation. The official interviewing him said, "I travel a lot, and see interesting countries and people, I wine and dine, and lead a very full and active life. But I sell razor-blades. Are you prepared to lead such a life? Are you prepared to sell razor-blades?" Tony said No.

Once when I had it in mind to settle down into a useful career, I offered myself as a trainee cinema manager. I had managed a theatre, I had actually formed and managed a whole theatre company, I knew every operation in both a theatre and a cinema, and could have walked into such a job without even being a trainee. But at the interview certain things were stressed: the cinema manager in any district where this particular chain of movie-houses operated was a personage akin to a doctor, lawyer or justice of the peace, said the interviewing gentleman. The cinema manager was a guide, friend, and philosopher, a local character, a person of gentle judgment, refinement, and discrimination. I must realise that if I desired to become a cinema manager, I must undergo three years' training with them in order to obtain the necessary psychological depth to be able to maintain the high standard of cinema management the chain had established. I did not get the job, and I am not sorry, because obviously a certain dimunition of character was necessary to swallow this kind of talk without a murmur of protest. A cinema manager who regards himself as a local priest is a man sadly out of touch with reality, a man who has reduced himself in stature in order to fill the tiny hole of a small job. The problem of the manageress in the department store, the woman who told her best men to work faster, was the same as that of her abject underling, Rabbit: fear. She did not look frightened, as he did; but she was. The big store is founded on fear; and fear is the operative force for discipline in the middle ranks of the managers and executives. In one of the best-known chain store systems of the English-speaking world, the most miserable character is the branch manager. The profits of his branch are calculated to minute fractions, and the smallest dip in the graph of "sales" brings to the doorway the ominous figure of "the man from the Head Office". An under-manager holds to his job with the same ferocity as a man holds to life; and the tragedy of losing a job can, in these stunted circumstances, be the same as the tragedy of losing one's life in a lustier time and place where life is cheap. The rule of terror is the same in both cases. The cause of the terror varies only because the men are different. Certain types of subnormal can be terrorised simply by sharp words. They see a breach coming between them and the source of their security. A man who knows his security lies with God is less likely to be afraid than a man who believes his security rests upon a sales-graph.

All these concessions by man to the method of business

leave the men less than they were before. When a work is seen out of focus, either as better than it is or worse than it is, when it is seen from the wrong angle, as when the means and the end are entangled or forgotten or confused, men lose their integrity in doing it. And if human personality has to be stripped away in order to do it, those parts stripped off are the very things that make for manhood.

Few jobs can be more degrading than that of a journalist on a daily newspaper. The journalist hires out to the newspaper his perspicacity, quick-wittedness and his descriptive fluency. These are precious gifts and easily damaged. In many cases, they are. He may have to accept restrictions on his judgment and on his style for no higher motive than the "policy" of the paper. Truth he finds regarded as a relative concept. His most precious possession, his ideals, he may be obliged to abandon if he wishes to hold his post. The modern newspaper proprietor buys not only a man's body but his ideals as well. This is not simply a matter of accepting the restrictions which any craft or art places upon the artist. Restrictions based on the form and the necessity for improvement are not only permissible but essential. But restrictions imposed by the whims of a man serving lesser interests, which deny a man the rational access to higher interests, are clearly immoral. When an employer, in the pursuit of the low goal of profit, causes a man, as he can do by economic pressure, to abandon his ideals, his morality, and his artistic integrity, he is not only trying to force that man to become a moron, he is proving himself a moron.

I worked on and off for years on a daily paper and for Catholic weeklies. Frankly, I say that news value has nothing to do with anything but the sales of the paper. Ethics of any sort are unpopular in this business, and the man who can salvage his integrity and his sanity from this kind of work is a fortunate and courageous man. I was fortunate in working for a daily paper which had some self-respect. I remember a great occasion when a leading scientist, a director of a research institute, gave an address on diphtheria immunisation. This was real news because his words, in a very real sense, might mean life or death to someone. I was given a half-column on the leader page, but my work-mates on other papers were not so fortunate. Their stories were butchered to sensational and uninformative paragraphs. The reader is familiar enough with the quality of daily papers to know that, with a few notable exceptions, what is printed is probably untrue, and that the real news of the day is probably not printed at all. There is of course the great quantity of material used which is simply trifling or sordid, may or may not be true, but is given to readers for its entertainment value alone. I recall a case during the war when an army officer and a woman from one of the auxiliary services were charged with a most offensive form of public behaviour. The judge criticised the prosecution for bringing the charge as there was so little evidence, and a verdict of "Not Guilty" was returned on both parties. A local paper published a front-page picture of the humiliated girl, a picture which actually showed only too pathetically how she had tried to avoid the camera. The caption was a jeer. There are hundreds of stories similar to this, but they cannot be told now. The effect on a journalist is plain enough. He loses what ideals he has, loses too much of his sense of decency and integrity, and like the commonest labourer becomes simply a human machine for carrying out on behalf of others assignments which human dignity would forbid him to carry out were he working on his own behalf.

A Catholic paper I worked for was worse. Catholic papers sometimes are. Catholicism in commerce has been known to eclipse the most pagan businesses in the immorality of its dealings with the public and with its employees. The reason is of course clear: business men in the pagan world have no standard of ethics, so they must set up and abide by, however roughly, some form of business ethics. Churchmen in business already have a form of ethics, and so great is the general cleavage between religion and work that in business some of them don't bother to use any ethics at all. A Catholic paper once carried a theatre criticism of mine condemning a slick and popular play as grossly immoral. On the opposite page, they carried an advertisement extolling the pure freshness of this dirty little bedroom farce. I was often cautioned not to be too severe in my criticisms lest it cost the paper valuable advertising revenue. I remember one of the senior men giving me a long lecture one day on the licitness of accepting advertisements like this. No moral question involved, he said, simply normal business.

I do not suppose any professions appeal more to people with alleged "talent" than those associated with public entertainment. The glamorous life of a popular radio announcer is almost entirely taken up with reading to order, in glib and sophisticated tones, the exciting news of a new stomach pill. I have never known an atmosphere in which personal envy, hatred and slander had a freer hand than in a London theatre where the reigning stage queen was having a successful long run in a foul American melodrama. The theatre is a fascinating art, but I would never work in it simply as a profession. It produces the most hatefully artificial relationships between people, and if, as is usual, the only criterion is commercial success, pulp and obscenity take over and the employee has to conform or lose his job.

To be a teacher is exasperating for the man and bad for the child unless one has the will, the vocation to be a teacher: to know, that is, what teaching is, why it is necessary, and to want to teach; to want to "do" teaching rather than to seem a teacher; to want to clear up the chaos of a youngster's mind and to restore order and harmony to it in spite of all difficulties or impediments. It is because so many teachers do not clarify these issues first that they become such strange people. To be a social worker is frustrating for the man and terrifying in its consequences to the client unless one wants to "do" social work for the right reasons—to love the poor, the friendless and the troubled so much that one is impelled to help them by whatever means available. Nursing, the trade of Florence Nightingale, is a filthy business unless seen for what it really means. Nursing is probably the dirtiest, most unromantic, unglamorous, most sordid and squalid of all occupations, if viewed only in terms of the actions performed. But viewed against the backdrop of human suffering, human souls, and human love, it is one of the noblest of all professions. A girl cannot hope to be a nurse if she thinks of herself solely as a heroine standing centre-stage, dispensing relief. She must actually want, for the love of an old man, to help that old man perform a number of functions necessary to his comfort, but of which young girls other than nurses are hardly expected to know anything. The nurse, for the love of that old man—no other motive would have the necessary force—must do things for him in his second childhood which his mother alone did for him in his first.

It is obvious enough in these occupations where the idea of "vocation" still persists. But vocation is simply the work to which one is called, and a good man can make a vocation from any work of integrity; and even in some cases, a very good man can drag a work that has lost its integrity back on the right path again, as did my friend in the clothing store. Work done in this fashion is work well done, and the personality thrives on it because work is the fertiliser of human personality. The desire to seem something, because it turns the ambition towards self, because it separates what one is from what one does, involves only a clash with reality. It is the mark of the dreamer, or the sufferer from delusions. Man needs more than that which will satisfy only his vanity. His being demands action. And what he does must depend upon the man himself, and not upon the prevailing standards of snobbery, class-consciousness, and social convention. If a man does not see his work as a method of doing something in a larger scheme of things, if he sees it simply as a vehicle for getting money, security, status, or any other of the lesser things, if he sees his work only in terms of self, that man becomes a moron, however superficially successful he seems to be. He becomes moreover a more dangerous moron, because his powers of judgment have not been destroyed, but have simply been twisted away from right ends to evil ends. Such men, as Caesar said, are dangerous.

V

THE BREAKDOWN OF BUSINESS

THE EMPHASIS on seeming rather than on being, the preoccupation with self, is the reversal of reason. And this has only become possible because our industrial philosophy has reversed reason on a much grander scale. The facts of industry as they stand are evidence of a moronic state of mind among those who frame our social philosophy at its most influential level.

The argument used to justify the employment of men in a manner that may make morons of them is twofold: first, that it benefits the employer because it "pays"; second that it benefits the employee and society by raising the material standard of living.

If both these propositions could be upheld in their entirety, they would still not justify the appalling and admitted decline in the spiritual and cultural life of society which even the capitalist as philosopher is as quick to admit as to disown responsibility for. But the propositions are worth examining. The more important claim is that capitalist industrialism does raise the material standard of living. Let us see if this is true.

Man has three basic needs: shelter, food, and heat. His other needs are either secondary, like education, or subdivisions of one of the primary needs, like clothing. I will not go into the matter of housing in detail. It is obvious that under industrial society, man has been less adequately housed than at any other time in history. The English Midlands will satisfy any sceptic of that. The peasant had a cottage and the goatherd had a hut, and at least the air was clean about both. Even the caveman had some property rights over his cave. Industrialism provided, first, dirt. Secondly, it took away home-ownership, erected the ominous figure of the landlord who was not even the lord of land but simply the owner of buildings and land; it took away privacy and added the danger of disease. When the public conscience became uneasy, the inventors discovered flats, chromium and pre-fabrication. It seemed as if their ideal was a Mongolian yurt, made of collapsible tin instead of horsehide, which the nomadic workman of today could unbolt and take with him on his endless journeying for work. Houses like this are of course some improvement on the houses of the preceding hundred years, but they are no improvement on the housing standard of history in general. Even in its efforts at reform, industrial housing has been pretentious rather than practical; and so delicately balanced is the problem of housing in a modern city that two wars are more than enough to throw whole populations into confusion and to turn every industrial city into a congested heap of human beings.

The rate of home-building in an industrial city never keeps abreast of the population increase. Consequently every industrial city tends to become congested. Out of congestion comes the tenement civilisation. The chief features of the industrial city are flats, apartments, and slums. All three are innovations resulting from industrial progress. Admittedly dirty squalid little houses have always existed, but the industrial slum house has a character of its own. The existence of hot water, central heating, air conditioning and de luxe washing machines may be cited as advantages only when they are as universal as the evils they are supposed to remedy. At present, the people who need them most are those who can least afford them.

It is essential to the dignity of man that he own his house, because he cannot properly make a home unless the ground and buildings are his to do what he likes with. Industrialism has slaughtered the owner-occupier. It is too difficult to obtain land because of concentrated populations. There is plenty of land in Australia, especially west of Alice Springs; there is even land for sale in England, but most of it is "too far" from work. In a natural civilisation, a man owns his house and land, and works on it. He stands proudly on his own two feet. The conventions of commerce today prevent him from being an independent workman, and so he must perforce file himself away in an approved house from which somebody draws a rent profit, so that he may sit, and not even proudly, at someone else's workbench. Modern man owns nothing. He cannot build a house himself because custom, local laws, and the widespread racketeering known as "normal business" require that he must hire another to build it for him. I know a half-dozen men who have competently built themselves better houses than any they could have obtained from the "building industry". But they stand alone. Building inspectors, health inspectors, sanitary inspectors, trade unions, and of course the neighbours have all descended on them ferociously for not conforming to pattern. In many areas, local councils decree the material from which the house is to be built, thus enforcing a filing-cabinet uniformity. My own house in Melbourne is in a "brick" area. In such an area a spurious imitation is permitted, such as brick veneer, because appearances count more than anything. But better building, as in stone or pise-de-terre, is not. None of the ancient classic methods of simple home-building which have been proved over the centuries to be the cheapest and best and simplest methods of all, is permitted by law in the city of Northcote, Victoria, Australia, and I understand that they have simply copied their standards in this, as they have copied their standards in everything else, from the established customs of the English-speaking world.

Michael F. built himself a two-storey house on a farming site in Victoria. He had never built a house before, and he would not have built one then had he not needed a place in which his wife and babies could live. His land was deep in the bush, a long way from builders, and also a long way from inspectors. It took him about a year to build his house, working part-time with the aid of a youth, and tending his farm simultaneously. It was taking the building industry about the same time to build a stucco villa in Melbourne. Michael's house was built from solid slabs of sandstone, quarried on his own land, and has the durability of a fort. He was given a giant lot of red-stained fruit-cases by a neighbour who wanted to get rid of them, and Michael broke them up into slats and panelled the interior. He put in a spiral staircase which he hewed out of local logs. He made everything down to the door-handles, but he had to buy cement, a kitchen sink and a bath. They were the only items which actually cost money. Michael was an artistic young man as well as an adventurous one, and his house is not only a better house than average but also a more beautiful one. It is a show-place of ingenious, simple, functional architecture. It will probably last for centuries. He would not have been permitted to build it in any of the big cities.

One other aspect of industrial housing needs special reference. It has become ethically permissible to "invest" money in land; that is, to buy land not for the purpose of developing it, but of re-selling it when the artificial money value of it has increased. By the same standard it has become permissible to withhold the sale or use of land until the price rises, even though people are desperately in need of land on which to build homes. Outside my window as I write at this very moment is a glorious tract of vacant land plumb in the centre of the most grossly overpopulated city in the world, London. It is fenced off, and trespassers are warned away. Children, desperate for playing space in London, are denied access to it. It is covered with weeds. Nobody uses it, everybody wants it, but the owner is waiting until the situation is "favourable", so that he can "realise" on it. One could dwell on this form of dishonesty at length, but it is outside the scope of this work. It is enough to say that the whole system of land speculation, land agents, real estate agents, rents and landlords as refined by industrial society, has made the problem of living more difficult for the oppressed and the weak.

The industrial manipulation of the food supply is based on the same notion that human necessity can be made the occasion of profit and speculation. One fundamental example might serve as an illustration.

In the days when man was primitive, so they said, the man who reaped his harvest of wheat sifted the chaff away and crushed the whole grain to flour for bread. He, poor backward creature, did not know that the outer layer of the grain contained Vitamin B, the antidote to beri-beri, or that it contained certain quantities of Vitamin E and minerals. He did not know that there were few good alternative sources for these essential vitamins. He did not even known that the endosperm, the big kernel of the grain, contained starch which was good fuel for his body. The only thing he knew was that he ate the lot and remained healthy.

When all these interesting discoveries were made it was too much to expect that the normal healthy habits of man could not be turned to somebody's profit. Advertising soon convinced the housewife that white bread was better than brown. It looked better, so according to the criterion by which all things were judged in the nineteenth century, it must *be* better. The manufacturers took the outer layer and embryo away, leaving only the starch store of pure carbohydrate. This is good food up to a point. It is good fuel, all right, but too much of it causes constipation and indigestion. God made the wheat grain in a manner that had proved effective for centuries, for the carbohydrate store of the grain was balanced by the vitamin and roughage content of the outer layer and embryo. Certain common disorders immediately followed this doctoring of the grain. To offset these disorders the roughage and the vitamins were repacketed and resold as medicinal commodities, health foods or breakfast foods.

The mass-production of wheat made it necessary in the interests of commerce that it be stored over long periods. Whole wheat is difficult to store because it is so rich in living organisms that it may germinate in a matter of weeks. Wheat meal can be stored for longer periods, but white flour can be stored indefinitely and so can the endosperm from which it is made. Not even the bugs will touch it, and they are not usually fastidious. It is in effect a packet of starch.

Profitable though this may be to the comparatively few people engaged in this form of business, it can hardly be said that it is for the benefit of anyone else. When the whole wheat is subject to extra processing in order to deprive it of its most valuable ingredients, it is natural for the price of this degraded product to be higher than the price of the better article. By the time the detached ingredients have been resold as proprietary lines, the customer has paid through the nose many times over. He has, in short, been swindled. He is swindled again when wholemeal bread is presented to the public as a refined form of bread and at a higher price than the already artificially high price of white bread. The extension of this roguery is to be found in those forms of brown bread whose brownness is achieved by artificial colouring to make them seem even more refined still. They lack the essential ingredients, and include as extra ingredients only a dose of dye. Chemically-coloured bread, both white and brown, is quite common.

This is a cake and pastry civilisation. It would need a dietician to comment adequately on the things people are asked to eat by advertising men, but the subject need only be debated when one serious medical man can be found to say that we eat sensibly, or even that our standard of eating has improved over the last hundred years. We are riddled with indigestion, flatulence and constipation, deficiencies and stomach disorders, because we eat so much rubbish that is nicely tinned or packeted, and tantalisingly offered by an ingratiating advertiser. And always in its train comes the remedy: the health food, the laxative, the liver salts, the cleanser, the scourer, the patent medicines, and the tonics. Are we really so sick that we need all this to straighten out our corroded insides in this century of the triumph of science?

Shelter, food and heat. I have already given you a note on how readily business supplies firewood to poor people when it can get twice the price on the black market. But there is another aspect of this. When my father built our present modern home in Northcote, Victoria, the architect left no place for the old-fashioned wood-stove. We had always had a wood-stove as well as a gas-stove, because all the houses we had lived in were old enough to have had a wood-stove in the first place. When the gas-stove was eventually moved in, the old wood-stove became a cupboard or a small addition to the pantry. So it seemed quite in order that a house built in the palmy days of 1939 before building became almost impossible should have only one stove and a gas-stove at that.

That was all right for a time. Then the New South Wales coal-miners became tired of hewing coal and the supplies became smaller and smaller. Supplies of gas also became smaller and smaller. And in the year of grace 1948, our old housekeeper, Florence Kirkham, faced with a de luxe gas-stove useless because there was no gas, found that in our streamlined house there was not even a fireplace where she could cook. So she went out into the garden and built a camp-fire like a pioneer woman of the Roaring 'Fifties, and cooked our Sunday dinner out there. The whole supply of domestic gas had become such a complicated and delicate piece of organisation that any breakdown on the path to our stove from the bottom of N.S.W. coal-mines meant we got no gas. Plenty of people have known not only un-cooked meals but plain cold since the war. The reason is partly but not entirely the cupidity of business men who have diverted the limited supplies to the most profitable goal; the reason is also because industrial society can become so complex, and therefore so artificial, that a tiny breakdown in the web of men and machines can cause widespread failure of an essential service. It becomes difficult to regard even electricity as a certain and constant friend when one man can plunge a city into total darkness by pulling a switch.

The degree to which human society has suffered at the hands of this philosophy is more properly the subject of a large and separate treatise. It is too vast a subject, too extensive a catalogue to deal with here in anything but the briefest outline. It is important now to consider the other proposition: that it can be justified because it "pays".

This argument is not one used by scrupulous men; but many business men will declare that business is business and the serving of Mammon really is a worthy goal. They will deny that there is anything unethical in selling dyed and gassed water as a drinking beverage at great profit to themselves. Because there is a great profit—in money, that is—they will counter protest with the defence that it is good business.

The argument can be met without bringing in the moral question. "Profit" is the amount left over after the investment of capital and the application of work to that capital. As a rule, business men omit from the balance-sheet the most valuable things they have invested in the business. A profit must be the return in greater quantity of what has been invested. If a business man invests not only money, but security, capacity to love and be loved, his powers, ability and capacity to create, his virtues and his physical strength—if he gives all these away and receives back only a slightly larger amount of money, then clearly his profit is a myth. When the more valuable things have been lost altogether there is no ground for boasting that one of the lesser things has been returned with a slight margin to spare.

In order to show that an investment really "pays", the business man must show that the project is managed with efficiency and economy; that the concealed losses are negligible; that he himself emerges not only richer in money but richer in other things as well. In the light of these considerations it is apparent that modern business methods do not pay. Modern business methods have produced a structure of inefficiency and waste, in which the bare margin of money profit won by those at the top is in striking contrast, not only to the losses inflicted upon others, but also to the real injury inflicted upon themselves.

This injury most commonly takes the form of destruction of the moral sense, and a childlike preoccupation with utterly unimportant things. These two characteristics are well-known symptoms of mental deficiency: the moron is generally amoral and he certainly gets most of his fun from the world of his delusions.

I will quote some more Australian examples; and it must be remembered that Australia is not an industrial country in the full meaning of the word. The disastrous growth in numbers of the white-collar worker has already been shown, but the meaning of the word "production" requires further analysis.

There are sixteen classifications of industrial manufacture. One is "Food, Drink, and Tobacco", and it employs the second largest number of people of all the industrial groups. The plants average a high percentage of employees, which points to the existence of large and centralised industrial activity. The total number employed was 105,878, the number of working proprietors, 3,969. In these and later cases quoted, the actual figures are not as important as the proportions.

Food production is the oldest of all industries, so it

cannot be said that industrialism has given the world something new. Since it is a primary need, it is not surprising that it employs a large number of people. A critical examination of what all these people are doing, however, will of course be controversial. But if we allow that urban populations need certain large-scale food services, it is possible to say that a certain number of industrial processes are necessary. There must be a certain number of factories. Remember that even in the largest of cities, a very considerable proportion of the food supply, such as vegetables and dairy produce, come to the consumer without industrial intervention. But factories are necessary for such things as flour-milling, corn-crushing, sugar-refining, butter-making, meat- and fish-preserving, ice and refrigeration, and salt manufacture. A count of the people engaged in that which seems necessary to the food supply of big cities gives us a figure of 36,382 persons. What about the other 69,498?

They are all engaged in factories, on processes which were once performed in the home, or which create only novelties, appetisers, or artificial tastes. The first class—industries once performed in the home—includes baking, pastry-cooking, the making of biscuits, confectionery and jams, fruit- and vegetable-canning, preserving and pickling, curing and sauce-making. The housewife used to provide all these things for herself. Now, for the most part, she buys food in a tin, or in cellophane, and complains that she is busier than ever. The second class of process, numerically far less important but still significant, includes the making of condensed and dried milks, the legitimate use of which is far less than the number of persons employed warrants; aerated waters, cordials, dehydrated fruits and vegetables, which also have a limited use; breakfast foods by the score; ice-cream and confectionery novelties.

Admittedly these have some value, but we ask simply that a sense of proportion be observed. In Australia, during the war, the manufacture of ice-cream was prohibited because it was believed that ice-cream was not truly essential. Ice-cream is appetising, but I do not think that any sane man will say that it is a staple food. When the American forces arrived, the ice-cream factories had to be reopened because ice-cream was a staple food for the Americans. In the front line the Americans received supplies of ice-cream because it was "essential", but the Australians did not. None the less, the Australians were very envious; and their opinion of the Americans was violently expressed. From the numbers employed in these industries we might reasonably conclude that such foodstuffs were very important; we also know, in reason, that they are not. We can only conclude that there is something wrong with our sense of values.

Of course there is. Over two-thirds of those engaged in the second-biggest industrial group are either replacing the normal artistry of the housewife with low-grade commodities, or catering exclusively for an artificial demand. The latter is more foolish but not so tragic as the former. A housewife is a potential artist. A factory-worker, engaged in fulfilling the same end less efficiently, does not represent progress. She who might have graced her family hearth and complimented her husband's stomach with a variety of products devised and created in her own kitchen workshop, now spends her entire working life making perhaps one part of one cheap bun in somebody else's factory. The art of the individual has been destroyed, and the work reduced to a level fit only for the lowest of intelligences. The product is worthy of the method of its manufacture.

Notwithstanding that men should be fed, clothed and housed, all of which is done with some difficulty under our present economic system, the manufacturing group which employs the greatest number of individuals is that classed as "Industrial Metals". Secondary food production employs 105,000 odd; "Industrial Metals" employs 292,477 persons—nearly three times as many. It is a conglomerate group:

Plant and machinery	46,123
Government transport vehicles	36,962
Motor repairs	21,012
Sheet metal working	18,114
Electrical machinery	22,825

are the principal sub-groups. Economic goods are of two types: "Consumer Goods" which are those that go to the customer, the ultimate consumer; and "Production Goods" or "maintenance" goods, which are useless as an end in themselves but are essential to the production of consumer goods. That is, simply stated, tools.

In a properly balanced economy, tools are an important but auxiliary section of industry. Unlike other types of manufacture, the making of these "production goods" has to be grouped in the "distributive" rather than the "productive" section of economic life. The vast army engaged in this group conforms to the vast army of middlemen generally.

Some comparison of the number engaged in these sub-groups with the number engaged in other more essential occupations is revealing.

Electrical equipment manufacture	28,825
Wool and weaving industries	7,253

I know all about Bradford and Lancashire, but I still say it is nonsensical. Australia is the greatest wool-producing country in the world, and in Melbourne's largest department store pure woollens were the most expensive of all clothing fabrics.

Industrial aspects of transport but not transport itself	124,060
Building and construction	84,152

We are at least looking ahead to nomadism. The number engaged in transport is so extraordinarily big that it must be looked at closely. There are more people in transport industries—that is, automotive equipment manufacture, servicing and maintenance—than there are engaged in the secondary phase of three basic needs of man.

Transport industries	124,060
Industrial food manufacture (analysed above)	105,878
Clothing manufacture	93,370
Building	84,152

To this must be added the almost equally large number engaged in actual transportation. An exact figure is impossible to obtain because it is statistically related to "communication". It is in the vicinity of 150,000. The reason for this curious disproportion was partly, if not fully, explained by a survey of the Ministry of War Organisation of Industry during the last war. An attempt was made to cut down long-distance commercial transport. The phenomenon discovered was labelled "cross-traffic". Reduced to simple terms, it means that too many men who live in Town A go to work in Town B, while too many men from Town B go to work in Town A; that is, they cross each day on their way to work. Similarly, goods manufactured in Town A are exported to Town B, while the same goods manufactured in Town B are exported to Town A. Because this suggests to the mind a myriad of goods and chattels meandering around the face of the earth in quest of buyers, it is very difficult to give compact examples. But the W.O.I. survey revealed that virtually all commercial transport could be eliminated without depriving the consumer of any real service. To be sure, the women of Melbourne might not be able to buy Shoes by Betty which were made in Sydney, and might have to stumble along on Shoes by Margaret which were made in Melbourne.

The economic radical who worked on this survey said that if Shoes by Margaret were confined to Melbourne, the reduction in cost made possible by the elimination of nation-wide advertising and transport would bring down the price of the shoes to something within the reach of a much greater number of women. And since, for the most part, Shoes by Margaret are identical with Shoes by Betty, everyone would be the gainer by such a simple solution, including the shareholders of both organisations. His recommendation was not accepted by the industrial barons who advised the department. They said it would interfere with the "liberty" of "normal business methods".

The underlying principle of the increased cost which capitalism hands over to the community is discussed at greater length below. For if this complexity, cross-traffic and advertising, huge overheads and elaborate costing was so well organised that the finished product was in fact cheaper for the consumer, we could thank capitalism for the service it does even if we deprecate its methods. But it does not seem so. The classic example of over-specialisation is Australian wool. The wool comes by waggon from the grassland to the railhead, is railed to a port, shipped to England, woven into cloth, shipped back to Australia. By the time it gets back to Bourke where the shearer lives, the shearer has to make do with cotton from Egypt because wool from Bourke is too expensive.

The wood industries throw more light than any other on the nature of industrial "progress". This group includes forestry, saw-milling, joinery, box-making and carpentry to the highest degree of fine cabinet-making. Historically, these industries are among the oldest known to man. One of the earliest recorded examples of wood-working was the making of the Ark.

Woodworking reveals more clearly than any other craft the fallacy of mass-production. The additional cost of the mass-produced article does not have to be demon-strated by subtle argument. It stands out on the price ticket. Some years ago, a Melbourne home-craft maga-zine sponsored a stunt offer to readers, called "pattern-made" furniture. The magazine supplied paper pat-terns and cut-timber for the reader to make his own furniture. Blazed across one of their advertising bills was the tactless remark: "This chair would cost you £10; make it for 30s."

This was a harsh betrayal of the furniture trade by one who was normally its friend. Until then buyers had paid their £10 for an arm-chair, with nothing but a complaint at the cost of living. When this advertise-ment appeared, some were curious enough to ask what happened to the other £8 10s. Pattern-made furniture soon disappeared from the reader's market.

The chair in question could have been made in less than a day, so the cost of labour would not exceed another 30s. That still left £7 unaccounted for. It goes of course to the various middlemen. A wartime survey of furni-ture-trades middlemen revealed that it was not uncom-mon for an item of domestic furniture to pass through five or six pairs of hands before its ultimate purchase by a harassed consumer. On an original cost to the manufacturer of £3, an agency fee of £1 would not be un-common. If there was only one middleman, that might be reasonable. With a veritable covey of wholesalers, agents, distributors, truck-drivers, advertising men, ware-housemen, and so forth, the final price bounces up to huge proportions.

Ralph Borsodi has discussed[1] the effect of the growing army of middlemen on the final quality and price of the article. A village carpenter (or any other craftsman) who supplies direct to his own community increases both his artistry and versatility by his personal contact with the customer. In addition, he can also reduce the cost by improving his workshop technique. His produc-tion expenses are low and his intelligence is applied directly to each assignment. The cost never exceeds that of his labour and materials. If this carpenter decides to mass-produce, he creates the same problems for himself as if I had gone in for firewood cutting on a big scale. Theoretically he can reduce the cost of each article, but he must look for a bigger market, and he must increase his overhead expenditure. Instead of supply following behind demand or keeping conveniently abreast of it, supply goes ahead of demand. This means more adver-tising to create the demand, and more middlemen to distribute the goods over the wider area. The cost of the article then begins to increase again. When the system has flowered over a century, mass-production is down to a fine art and the world is the market. Many sharp folk have found that being middlemen is more profitable and more secure than being manufacturers. In the end

[1] In *Flight from the City*.

the mass-produced article costs more than the craft-made article. Since it is also by definition an inferior article, it is difficult to see who is the gainer. It cannot even be said that the manufacturer is the gainer, for he has lost the joy of being a craftsman, he has enmeshed himself in a vast organisation of staff, costs, distributors, advertising and the constant fear of "losing his markets". He may have moments of prosperity, but it is purchased at a terrible price.

I myself have made to measure and to the exact specification of my client a set of book-shelves for £3, which he could otherwise only have obtained in standard, and therefore ill-fitting sizes, for £12. It did not have the frills and pretty trimmings which quantity tooling can provide so cheaply, but it served its purpose better, lasted longer, and at least looked more honest.

The craft of course disappears from woodwork when the workshop sells out to mass-production. I found one sample workshop making only ice-chests. They wanted to employ an apprentice because sometimes apprentices are the cheapest form of labour. They said they made two styles of ice-chest, but on being pressed for details, they admitted the two styles were obtained merely by switching a pattern. Identical processes were used on both models and an apprentice would learn nothing in such a place. It has now become commonplace for machine-morticing to replace good dovetailing; for strawboards to replace good plywoods in backing; for veneers to replace good timbers; and for such practices as artificial graining to replace fine polishing. In such an environment the work becomes sub-standard. So does the worker; and a sub-standard man is a moron.

The growth of the middleman is one of the strangest and most alarming phenomena in the economic history of man. A great proportion of the population is not engaged in productive work but is living on the work of others and necessarily increasing the cost of living for the consumer. This number cannot, of course, be accurately stated, because there are degrees of parasitism in various occupations which make statistics quite useless. An agent, or a middleman, is not *per se* parasitical. He becomes so only when there are too many of his kind. We can say that there are too many of his kind when his numbers almost equal those of the producers. But we cannot say of any particular agent or middleman that all his work or some part is necessarily parasitical unless we pinpoint the exact work done by a particular man at a given moment.

With certain extreme cases we can risk a general condemnation. There is on the "professional" level of society a type of middleman who has no intention of serving the community in any way but is content simply to live on it by a self-appointed occupation of no social usefulness at all. The classic example is the advertising man. To say that advertising is legitimate because its function is to advise consumers of available goods is to ignore the whole theory of modern advertising, which is the artificial creation of demand. This persuasion is, in almost every case, levelled at the vanity, cupidity or folly of the potential buyer. One person with delusions can, in favourable circumstances, infect others with those delusions. A person who believes himself to be Hannibal may not infect others because the improbability of such a claim being true is usually apparent, even to the most innocent bystander. But a delusion of usefulness, honesty and integrity is very infectious. Its delusory character is not so identifiable. It is well known that in ethical matters man has a natural tendency to accept the lowest common denominator rather than the highest; the high-pressure advertising man, being usually either a rogue or a sufferer from delusions, succeeds in either case in infecting others.

There are three major types of parasite work, and delusions are common to all. Two of them can, for convenience, simply be labelled "Pirate" and "Pervert". The third is not so easily labelled.

A "pirate" occupation is one concerned solely with making money at other people's expense. It is the logical end of the common business concept of self-supremacy. At its lowest level, it embraces the spiv, the sales shark, and the confidence man. At a higher and more respectable level, it includes the manufacturers of useless gadgets, novelty goods, goods which do not fulfil their function, goods with a spurious function. At an even higher level, there are those who steal trade names, or re-market old commodities under new names. If this is done with the bravado of a common burglar, it can be accepted for what it is. But when it is done with a sense of righteousness, it brings sanity under suspicion. The amorality of morons is well known. One pities them, but one does not trust them. A man who has lost his moral judgment is a pitiable person, to be cared for and loved certainly but never to be trusted. He has lost one of the most priceless parts of his intellect. There was a business magnate employed by the Ministry during the war, called Roger. Roger was receiving something like £1,000 p.a. for his patriotism. He was a large, noisy man who seemed very efficient and practical, but actually he had the same kind of industriousness as a magpie which loves to clutter its nest with odds and ends picked up from everywhere. Roger covered his desk with papers, and shouted, and ran about the passageways, but he made much more work for himself than he needed. He explained to a group of us over supper one night how, prior to the war, he had bought a certain well-known petroleum by-product, rebottled it with a new label, and marketed it as a cleansing solvent for twice the original price. He believed, and so did most of his colleagues, that this was simply "good business".

A "pervert" occupation is one of intrinsic social value which has, by the march of time and the evolution of commercial morality, been turned to evil ends. The best example which springs to mind is printing. Once upon a time books were rare because they always had to be copied by hand. The invention of printing was, at first, a notable step towards the intellectual improvement of humanity. The paradox is, of course, that "cultural progress" soon stopped. There is not much doubt now that the world was culturally better off when men could not read, and books were rare. Shakespeare and Christopher Marlowe were popular commercial playwrights in their own day, but they are so highbrow, so unpopular, and even so incomprehensible today that government subsidies are often necessary to maintain this part of our national heritage. Every one is "literate" in the sense that he can detect the obvious meaning of printed words. But during the war I waded through thousands of letters written by the Australian public at large and I will deny that they can write, either legibly or coherently. Being able to read is no advantage anyway, unless one reads the right things. In this day of easily available education and culture, a brief survey of a "popular" bookshop or newspaper-stall will revolt anyone of normal intelligence. Those who are not revolted by it are not of normal intelligence.

The "pirate" also operates extensively in this field. It is difficult to understand how, in the heart of the biggest city in the world, where Christian values are supposed to be the foundation of an intense public morality, sexually stimulating literature of the most beastly kind can be hawked in the most public of places. London's dirty bookshops and its nocturnal pavement stalls must be a novel sight for foreigners from "backward" countries. The statue of Eros in Piccadilly Circus was an appropriate choice.

The last type of parasite occupation is the one most difficult to name and on which to pass judgment. It may perhaps be defined as a useful service to useless clients. Take the example of an accountant: if finance, money-changing, profit-making, investments, taxation and forms of property had not become so complex, if they had not become the central concepts of the business world, accountants would not be necessary. And while they contain within their ranks their fair share of money-jugglers and profiteers, there are many who are men of professional honesty whose duty it is to serve a client helpfully and fairly. They are like guides to a deep jungle. They may approve the habits of the jungle or they may not but their work as guides is not affected.

I have mentioned only a few examples among the thousands of occupations which men have. And there would be no point in mentioning more, since many are so mixed in their social value. The window-cleaner is a useful friend to the busy housewife. He can be introduced occasionally to do a job in such a specialised manner that he takes away nothing of the artistic management of the housewife. But even this can become a racket. Window-cleaning was almost a major industry in London in 1950–1, and the window-cleaner, by becoming a wage-earning cog in a window-cleaning combine, was well on the way to losing his dignity and status as an honourable and useful workman. If you wanted your window cleaned it was often better to do it yourself than have it done by a mutinous and reluctant wage-earner.

It is all the same problem: production or work for profit cannot replace production or work for use and service. The concept of working for a living instead of living by a work not only debases the man by its refusal to regard him as a whole man; it produces inferiority and mediocrity in the product, and it makes life harder for everyone. I recall a shrewd boy with whom I was at school, and whose progress into "business" I watched with pain and anger. When I last saw him he was in the "blouse-making business". He was not making blouses. He knew nothing of how to make blouses. But he could talk glibly, and he had persuaded a number of young girls to make blouses for him and a number of shops to sell them, and he was making over £1,000 a year, doing nothing himself except talk. That he did so little himself was his proudest boast. He was "successful" in business. And yet he knew, and I knew, that his prosperity was a flimsy make-believe, for it was based on nothing real. If he employed girls to do his work for him, he knew that he was more of a slave than they were. The two unhappiest men I have ever known were millionaires. They thought they had everything they wanted, but they had nothing that their real selves wanted. They had tried to live by bread alone, and when that proved insufficient they had moved to a refined form of economic pastry, and they had gorged themselves until they were sick. They were sick of life because they had twisted the real things of life out of recognition. The rich commit suicide more often than the poor. The poor may suffer from reality, but that is better than suffering from make-believe. Those who believe that this form of "work" does "pay" are deluding themselves more than anyone else. The so-called successful millionaire is the greatest sufferer because he has thrown away most in his hot pursuit of the least profitable.

VI

THE MOTIVES OF MANAGEMENT

THE ORIGIN OF THESE widespread delusions is interesting and important. And it is by nailing down all these variously manifested errors of man to one general fallacy that we can see why the labourer is a potential moron, why the millionaire is an actual moron. Let us look at the very beginning of it.

Industry began when one man had to supply all his own needs. It became more complex when several men found they had different aptitudes, and could work together supplying their communal needs; so that everyone was better off by making or doing the things he could do best and then exchanging the products according to his needs. This was "production for use": the application of the aptitudes of one to the needs of another.

The philosophy of industrialism went deeper than merely misinterpreting the idea of "progress". It was not only as if this philosophy proceeded in a wrong direction. When it accepted as legitimate the idea of thinking first of oneself, it went backwards. Man had always known this rule of life to be the rule of the jungle. But when this very old, very primitive law of self-supremacy, with all its backward implications, was rediscovered by the economic theorists of the eighteenth and nineteenth centuries, there was something tragically sinister in the way mankind accepted it without a murmur of protest. Since the law of self-supremacy is unnatural to the whole nature of man, while being only too natural to the lowest part of his nature, it was bound to cause trouble. It did.

Industrialism substituted for the concept of "production for use", the concept of "production for profit". The kind of intellect which reduced the ambitions of man to this low level soon reduced the term "profit" to mean only material gain. It did not take long for material gain to come to mean money alone. Even applause and prestige became of less value than money; even land, the most valuable material thing a man can own, was reduced to the undignified category of a "frozen asset". Work came to mean—not simply for the usual selfish few but for everyone—the rendering of services or the making of goods for no motive higher than the acquisition of money for oneself.

As such, the quality of goods or services became of secondary importance. The principal aim of such work was to get the potential customer to accept them. So men began to confine their work to what was likely to yield the most money. The criterion of the excellence of work was reduced to the amount of money to be made from it. The beginnings of a new chaos can be seen here. It became right and proper for a man to grow richer and richer with no goal other than riches. It became right and proper for a man to own more and more property, real and personal, because it represented riches; it became right and proper, in order to do this, for a man already rich and powerful to delude the weak and innocent into surrendering their property to him. The consent of the weak became an argument in favour of aggression by the strong.

In other words, values came to be assessed in terms of money, the most valueless of all things. The excellence of an employment is now measured by the ratio of effort to pay envelope, and the excellence of management by the size of the profit. We have come a long way from the British guildsmen who forbade one craftsman to say publicly that his work was better than that of another craftsman; and even farther from the sword-makers of Damascus who summoned to trial the maker of an inferior sword and chopped his head off for betraying the standard of their craft.

At all levels, the only satisfaction now sought is that of the smallest and lowest part of man.

This fantastic worship of money has a violently stupefying effect upon the people who believe in it. A lunatic, after all, is only a person out of line with reality. It is not his deductions which are wrong but his premises. A man who leads a non-existent army into the asylum duckpond is acting logically, given that he believes himself to be Napoleon and the duckpond to be Russia. A man who believes that money is the most desirable thing to have in this world or the next, can behave very logically but with no less lunacy. A prominent violinist I knew once left a symphony orchestra to lead a commercial radio ensemble playing for a soap session. He had been offered a much higher salary because soap, these days, is much more profitable than symphonic music. That in itself is worth noting. When his action was criticised, a spokesman said in his defence that his new salary was so much higher that "he could not afford not to take it". The full enormity of that remark, as an expression of moral standards, takes time to sink in.

In London, during the war, the Germans did a fine job of slum clearance around Cheapside, and for the first time in centuries, Londoners at lunch could see St. Paul's, the sun and the sky. This open swathe of flattened ruin is now one of the most charming parts of London. Could it not remain so? asked the innocent. No, said the experts, the land is too valuable.

The idea of land values boxes up a lot of intelligences. A millionaire friend of mine once bemoaned the garden around Melbourne's oldest Catholic church in the heart of the city. "Wasted," he groaned; "some of the most valuable land in the city and all they put on it is a garden." He wanted to ring it with shops, and to confine the entrance to an alley-way. In London's East End, bomb sites became the first playgrounds children had had for years. It was unthinkable, growled the experts, to leave them to that purpose. The land is too valuable.

If, of course, money is to be the thing we worship, if Judas instead of Christ is to be the mentor of our moral life, it is quite rational that everything should be saleable. And indeed, for the most part, everything is: the body, the soul, the personality of man, the intricate beauty of human nature itself—all these things become simply commodities which can be sold or bought or even destroyed if sufficient pieces of silver are paid over by way of compensation. If a man breaks certain laws, he is permitted by law to buy his way out of punishment by payment of what is called a fine. If a man's reputation is ruined by the evil words of another, justice is presumed to be done if the offender pays over a price in money at which the damage to his character is assessed. By the ethical standards of business today Judas was irreproachable. His only weakness was his attachment to reality, and he saw in the end what the true values were. If he ended his life with what might be called a sentimental display of remorse, he preserved at least his sanity. The modern business man, abandoning reality for his delusions, saves his life by sacrificing his sanity. The application of his philosophy to the history of mankind shears out of human achievement almost every act of human nobility, courage, love, faith and heroism. Honour of course becomes meaningless. Man in short allowed himself to become a predatory animal.

Fair enough. If money is god, and man is a saleable commodity, then the parts of man are saleable too; but not in the true sense of service. There is nothing intrinsically wrong with one man working for another. The New Testament is full of analogies drawn from the master-servant relationship. The new concept of the saleability of man went further than that.

When Marx popularised the concept of the proletariat, he isolated a new concept of relationships. Proletarianism is not a master-servant relationship. The proletariat is that body of men, today the majority, who have ceased to be responsible workmen in any sense, and who have sold their human responsibility and such gifts as they possess, either in whole or in part, to a person of material wealth who wishes to use their resources to increase his wealth.

This is a wretched state of affairs. In most cases, the proletariat had no choice. The invincible greediness of the merchant class in the nineteenth century broke through the independence of the peasantry, forced them to become employees or starve. Today there are too many proletarians who prefer it that way. The merchants have trained them well over the century.

Marx recognised some of the iniquity of this, but his morose preoccupation with the material world denied to his undoubtedly great vision the full extent of the industrial tragedy. Marx saw only that by a combination of villainy and weakness, men could be enslaved by a new form of oligarchy. But the slavery, in his view, was only material, like the world he wrote about. Marx was a materialist and his view was a correct one so far as it went. It did not go far enough. Marx and the whole world movement which he instigated were not concerned with anything but the surface of the problem. It was not with the nature of riches that Marx was concerned but only with their distribution. Nor was it with the nature of work but only with its conditions. Marx swallowed the conventions of bourgeois capitalism like everyone else. Precisely because the root of the trouble was never touched, the old philosopher unleashed upon the world the same evil in a worse form—state capitalism for private capitalism, state proletarianism for private proletarianism. The trade unions, formed to defend man against the aggressor, finally accepted the aggressor's philosophy. Though they have softened at times the evil effect of the disease, they have at other times made it worse. The unions, representing the effort of the worker to solve the problems brought about by capitalism, have failed because they accepted this false interpretation of man. The unions swallowed the conventions, as Marx did. And being concerned only with a part of man, they have never been in sight of solving the real agony of the workman. To the extent that they too have endorsed the doctrine of self-supremacy, adopting for themselves the greed of their masters, they have made it worse.

When I worked in a kitchen, as I did at Cambridge, I cared very little for hours which were long or for pay which was low. I worked from 7.30 a.m. to 8.30 p.m., with two hours off in the afternoon, and I received my keep and 30s. a week. I did low-down skivvy work such as peeling potatoes and washing dishes. I enjoyed myself. Had I, like my friend, Tom C. at Oxford, been manager of a splendid hotel instead of assistant cook at a youth hostel, I would have been unhappy, as he was. He had to wear morning dress, poor devil, and behave himself. I wore shorts and an open-necked shirt and sang at my work in a most undignified fashion. It was he who had to live and behave like a flunkey, not I. A potato-peeler is a free and independent workman. The assistant manager of a big hotel is a slave.

Why? Because my work was worth doing and his was not. My job was to help feed hungry people as quickly and as cheaply as possible. My master was the hungry and homeless man; since I had ready for him the things he needed most, our relationship was human, cordial and wholesome. Tom's master was a more

147

subtle and domineering monster. The object of the hotel was not the satisfaction of human needs. Its object was to make money. It chose as a means to the making of money the ostensible satisfaction of human needs; but it could not confine itself only to satisfying real needs for then it would not make enough money. The non-profit-making hostel would be too serious a competitor. The hotel had to find, if necessary to invent, other needs to satisfy, and these included most of the "services" and luxuries so-called which distinguish the rich hotel from the plain little hostel: Tom's morning coat, the bowing and scraping of the liveried flunkeys, and the obsequious attentions of an army of maids and waiters. Such services are aimed straight at the self-interest of the client.

There is no cordial, wholesome or human relationship between two totally self-interested people. The one is out to make money by exploiting the desire of the other to show he has already made it. Tom knew there was something wrong with his job somewhere, but he may not have known exactly what. His master of course was not the management, nor the client, but the one thing that linked those two self-interested parties together—riches. Tom had tacitly endorsed the notion that riches, not even in the pocket but simply in the abstract, were worthy to be served. This master of course is merciless and inhuman.

Acting according to the law of the jungle—the law of self-supremacy—need not interfere with a man's sanity so long as he faces reality. A bad man is not a lunatic as long as he admits his badness. When the law of the jungle is adopted by a society which prides itself on its gentleness of behaviour and sublimity of social standards, then the genial idiocy of the moron becomes painfully evident. Rather than hit one's customer over the head and rifle his pockets, which would be the logical thing to do, the man of business preserves the externals of civilised behaviour by fanning up the self-interest of his customer to the point where the money changes hands. Payment for flattery is mutually satisfying, and the necessity for tooth and claw is avoided. There is something idiotic about two men of business, both determined to get the most they can by giving the least in return, treating each other with affable joviality, Dale Carnegie courtesy, and inviting each other to dinner. Such behaviour lacks even the little dignity left in the method of tooth and claw.

Marx's solution to this problem would have been to make me assistant manager of Tom's hotel and put Tom into the hostel kitchen for punishment. It would not have been a satisfactory solution. It is much more reasonable to find out what man really wants. The understanding of the true needs of man is the key to the integration of man; and they cannot be understood unless we know what man is. Not even Marx thought that elementary question worth trying to answer.

VII

THE MUTILATION OF MAN

MAN IS A member of the animal kingdom, sub-kingdom of vertebrata, of the class of mammals, and the order of primates. But this description of a backboned, breast-fed, vertical biped does not give us the whole picture. Man is not only an animal.

If he were he would be content at his work. He would be incapable of some of his greatest acts of apparently irrational heroism, and he would certainly be incapable of some of his more common acts of beastliness. A horse is incapable of wisdom or worry. A monkey has no clear notion of charity and hates only the things which hurt it. Man can hate the things which love him. He can pray for those who persecute him, and he can be a martyr for what he believes in. A bullock can do none of these things. A Tibetan yak, a hunting-dog or a domestic cow is the most patient of working creatures. Man's reaction to work is complicated, sensitive and unpredictable.

The parts of man with which he may work well are so numerous that it is impossible to make a complete list. His body, its strength and senses; his knowledge, judgment, ability to love; his will, emotions, and intuitions are all potential tools of his work. And his simplest act is a complex one. A watchdog fulfils its purpose without knowing what its purpose is. But a watchman cannot fulfil his purpose without the use of senses, judgment, experience, memory, knowledge, and the power of self-directed movement. The difference between a hunting-dog and a hunter is infinite. A horse can carry heavier loads than a human horse, but a human horse is called upon to make the most precise decisions. The difference between a four-legged horse and a human horse is that a horse can pull a heavy load but is not the judge either of its load or its direction. A human horse can pull one load and push another, can steer the latter while steadying the former, and may be required to exercise the most careful judgment as to the route to be taken through a traffic jam of congested barrows. And unwilling though a horse may be to work, its skill at evading work is not a fraction as refined as the skill and cunning with which an unwilling human horse can evade work.

Man has furthermore a conscience, a judgment of what is right and wrong. It may be a poor judgment founded on inadequate knowledge, but it is there all the same and it insists upon guiding his actions. A working bullock is as untroubled by moral considerations as a tractor.

Because both the hunter and his dog are fully alive, all their parts function together. The repression of one part will create a fury of unrest in the other parts, which, though not perceptibly restrained, are nevertheless inhibited by the overt restraint placed upon one part. And this indirect repression of some parts by the direct suppression of others is called frustration.

It is a painful experience. Man and dog can more readily accept confinement if it is apparent to their senses. They can acquiesce in what their perceptions tell them to be reality. But a confinement by frustration is like an invisible wall into which they crash repeatedly and which they may not understand. An invisible barrier is more painful than a visible one, not only because of the shock of the impact but also because of the tension between intellect and reality. One is up against something not fully understood, and therefore not fully remediable by rational judgment.

Frustration is an overworked word but unfortunately it is the only word. And it is of course the key to the moronising effect of contemporary work.

There is one curious form of work in which all men seem to find some contentment; that is, cleaning up. Even in the paper mill, the one job which united all in a cordial cohort of energy was that done with the brooms. In a department store, the bored and listless salesman could jump with glee upon a corner of chaos and could be made happy by the orderly stack which appeared under his busy hands. Children, the most wilful of creatures, can be bribed unscrupulously by the offer of being allowed to "tidy up". One day in the toyshop two small girls who came in to buy cards were depressed by the condition of the card cabinet. They actually volunteered to restore order. For two hours they were lost in the task of sorting out five hundred cards, and when they were finished, both they and the cabinet shone with happiness. There are many people who even find cleaning out a pigsty a source of tremendous joy.

This love of cleaning, tidying and ordering is so

universal in all people of all ages that there can only be
a profound reason for it. For man can derive a huge
enjoyment from making things, and of all things the
easiest to make is order from chaos.

All forms of making are evolved from this desire to
make order from chaos. It may be to make a useful chair
from useless wood, it may be the making of peace between
warring factions, it may be the making clear of a complicated proposition, it may simply be the making
accessible of a chaotic corner of the room or of the
mind.

There is chaos, and the nature of man seeks to make
order from it. The existence of one and the possibility
of the other are two things that must be made quite
clear. Familiarity with local disorder may, indeed does,
blind the eye of the speculator to the existence of universal
chaos in man, in nature, in everything. The sooner the
existence of that chaos is seen, the sooner man can begin
intelligently to do something about it.

Obviously if order is to be made from chaos, it must be
done with order itself. The bigger the mess, the more
need for precision in the plan to clean it up. And this
chaos is not simply an untidy corner which can be swept
away with a hard stroke of a broom. There is subtlety
in this chaos, and man may even need to be cunning
in his attack. Right order is essential. The nature of
man is so complex that the slightest misdirection of his
energy, the slightest lack of an essential ingredient throws
the whole sensitive machinery of his composition into a
mangled fury of dissatisfaction. Just as sex without love
produces beastliness, so work without knowledge of its

end produces forms of animalism more varied and more obdurate than that of the most mutinous farm animal.

The first work was done by God when He, being love, allowed His love to overflow into the creation of angels, men and matter. His finest work of creation was to unite spirit and matter in man. Man in the full glory of his sinless paradisal state was called to work by God: to be God's gardener. In that state he was able to contemplate God freely and fully and his life was in complete tune with the fountain of beauty. Because he was a perfect man he was called to work, to add, that is, creation upon creation; to enrich and to build; to praise God not only with his mind but also with his hands. The morning prayer of Prime expresses it better:

> Look down upon thy servants O Lord
> and upon the works of thy hands
> and direct their offspring;
> and let the glorious beauty of the Lord our God
> be upon us,
> and direct thou the work of our hands
> over us.

Adam being proud and Eve being wayward wanted more, and at the suggestion of the serpent they fell away from God and were henceforth obliged, Adam to work by the sweat of his brow, Eve to suffer in her children. The world was plunged into this disorder and chaos we know so well.

The restoration of order from this chaos is the task

of the worker, and only by knowing this does man regain some of his lost integrity, that is, the right relation of his smallest part to the ultimate end of his whole.

Rationally man knows where his integrity lies. It would not be sufficient only to contemplate God, because his body would not be playing its part as well. In the paradisal state that intellectual knowledge of the beauty of work would be sufficient. Body and soul would combine joyously to praise God by adding creation to prayer. But in the fallen state the beauty of creation becomes subordinate to the necessity for restoring order from chaos. Intellectual knowledge of this in the fallen state is not enough to get it done. The will is at war with the intellect, the body is at war with the soul, and man, body and soul, finds nature at war with him. And it is part of the marvellous design of God that man, by the now insistent obligation to work, can carry on, though in an imperfect fashion, the original work of praising God with body as well as soul. (Because of the disruption between the parts of man and between man and nature, man cannot survive without working; without, that is, restoring order. In doing so, he can also praise God.) In his fumbling manner, he is forced for his own sake into doing what his first parents did only for God's sake. If he can see this higher function of work his life becomes fuller and richer, and he lifts himself by the sheer doggedness of his spiritual will out of the slough of Adam towards a glimmering resemblance of the paradisal state.) And thus, it may be argued, he becomes more dear to God by his effort at love, by his determination to defeat the handicaps imposed on him by his first parents, and by the achievement of so infinitely more difficult a task.

Work is an act of love. It is an act of manhood, in all the spiritual as well as the material meanings of the term. Work is an act of courage and strength. Work brings man closer to God and is therefore divine.

Potentially, that is. The energy of all men has for its natural goal the restoration of order from chaos, the restoration of all things to God to whom they belong. But not all see it that way. The best of us see it only "through a glass darkly". Too many do not see it at all. We see only human energy demanding outlet. If this colossal generation of power does not find its real channel, then a frightful frustration, comparable with that of a caulked-up volcano, is the result.

The body alone can achieve a form of contentment by doing almost anything. The energy of the body is absorbed by action, regardless of what the action is. The body can eat, sleep, go to fun fairs, read comic papers, watch the cinema, or plod through a shiftless daily task, and it can become quietly, bovinely content. But man is body and soul, and only when he is engaged upon the sanctifying work of restoration is he living a fully human life: living that is, in full accord with his function and nature as a man. His body is satisfied by its activity, his intellect by the nature of what is being done.

Between these two extremes—the body seeking only the most primitive satisfactions and the intellect seeking the highest of satisfactions—the other parts of man fall easily into their right place. Interfere with this balance between the two extremes and you interfere with the right working of man.

The trouble with industrial employment is that it has never attempted to discover what it hires when it hires a man. The theorists blandly said that labour alone was the commodity traded when a worker signed on the payroll. But that is manifestly untrue, as every worker who has been carpeted for "not using his intelligence", will know. My term as a porter ended because the manageress thought that a sense of responsibility was one of the things I contracted to supply when I was engaged to carry parcels. In a grotesque way the industrial employer imagines that he can hire a part of a man, while still obtaining at his convenience the use of the other parts as well if he wants them. He wants the whole man to be at his disposal even if for the time being he is content to immobilise, either indirectly by the nature of the work or directly by the discipline of the organisation, the parts he does not want immediately. Sometimes he asks for more. One shop in London actually had a rule that their "partners" were forbidden to earn any extra money from outside sources, even during their free time. If they wanted to engage in profitable work in their own time they had to ask permission. This rule extended the ownership of the worker outside even working hours. The rule was of course arrogant, and unenforceable; and it was rightly ignored by most of the workers who had outside interests. It may have fooled some of the workers; I do not know. Whether he hires an employee for his intellect, his strength, his wit, or his senses, the employer does not hire the whole man as such. He hires only a "hand", or an "operative", or at best, some "brains". He accepts benignly, as his right, the free gift of the whole man who has necessarily to accompany his dutiful faculties to work.)

Employers are content to employ parts of men because they imagine that it will cost them less, and because they hope to order this raw material more satisfactorily to their own ends. Chain stores like to get their managers young. In certain chain stores, the employee is not just a man who works there; he is a special type of man, taken as by the Comprachicos at childhood, and deformed for the purposes of the cult during his impressionable years. They do not always succeed, because those unpleasant people used a knife and knew what they were doing, wicked though it was, whereas the modern employer is not sure what he is doing and is certain only that it is right and normal. But the evil is impressed in some form from the beginning.

The unwanted faculties have two miserable courses to choose. They may lie in disuse, atrophy and die altogether. Or in sheer desperation or innocence, they may be given voluntarily to the service of the employer. If the work itself has integrity, this free gift of faculties not purchased by the employer may yield a good result. The personality of the worker may be strong enough to assert itself and to survive. In the two-man toyshop, for example, this was possible. The nature of the work was wholesome enough. The corruption was only in the human element, and fortunately this was recognised by the master. My most common complaint was that I had not been purchased in my entirety. Since my employer owed at least a nominal allegiance to the principle that slavery was immoral, he had to find some other way of getting the maximum use out of me, and my wits were as good as his. He had to admit that I reserved some rights, and my most precious right was the assertion of human dignity in giving him without payment the most useful faculties I had because I preferred them to be used for something rather than not to be used at all. In the nature of the work I could not use them for myself. They had to be abandoned or given to him. This kind of thing frequently happens; it is the normal sign of a conscientious employee who likes his work, and it is a pity employers do not express more gratitude for being so treated rather than so much indignation when they are not so treated. If the work itself has no integrity, then there is little alternative to mutilation. The granting of the unwanted faculties cannot satisfy the worker because in giving them to avoid disuse, he accepts their misuse. His only chance of avoiding mutilation is to withdraw as much of his self from the job as he can, to accept the suffering involved and to hope that the demands made upon him can be met by enough to hold his job and his sanity. Sometimes he cannot hope to hold both.

The postal sorter, for example, applied all his mental faculties to his work. This was not work for an intellectual giant, but the intellectual demands made required at least a normal healthy man. His body, unwanted and disused, could do as it liked. It could accept, and did, the confinement necessitated by physical presence and it could adjust itself accordingly, reserving full compensation for Saturday afternoon on the football field. Had any postal official told the sorters to sit, or to stand, to stop slouching, or to put their feet down, the job would have been intolerable. Had they been told to put their coats on, or to stop smoking, they might have walked out. If there had been a clear reason for any of these instructions, the additional restriction would have been accepted willingly; but to obey such instructions merely at the whim of the master would be to surrender a part of human personality. Such instructions can only be carried out by something akin to mutilation. Mutilation can solve the anguish of frustration up to a point, it can bring a form of contentment; but it is a wicked form purchased at a wicked price.

In the paper mill, the price of contentment was mutilation of the conscience to make it accept laziness and indecency, and of the intellect to make it accept the application of so much that was good to so much that was bad. In the department store, contentment was possible if one accepted the morality of sales methods and the regimentation of the body. To the public service clerk, contentment came as it comes to a cow in the field, to him whose mental faculties could be artificially slowed down to the point where simple transcription was enough to consume all his energy. On the other hand, the goodsyard labourer was happy enough if he had something with which to occupy his mind. If he made no attempt to look after his mind, it would certainly become corrupt through inactivity; that was his own responsibility.

There is nothing intrinsically wrong with employing

a part of a man only. (But because a physical job may reduce a man to an irresponsible clod, there is a strong case against any society which increases the number of physical jobs beyond the limit of the number of men who can safely undertake such work. Physical work is greatly underwritten by modern standards, but one of the curses of the white-collar worker is that there is nothing physical about his work at all. It is not without strong reason that the Benedictine rule requires a period of manual labour every day, for every scholar recognises the intimate relation between manual labour and intellectual work. Because manual labour leaves the mind free, the mind may turn to waste or to God.) But the mind is a turbulent and restless thing and needs intense discipline. If he can apply this discipline, the manual worker has a good chance of preserving his sanity. Less of him is required than in any other job. If the nature of his work is such that his other faculties can be freely directed by him into worthy channels, he can remain a whole man. But if he lives in a pagan atmosphere, absorbing pagan influences, then the very inactivity of his mind is his worst handicap. In a civilised community, the physical labourer, especially the farm labourer, would be rightly regarded as the most fortunate member of society. One must face the fact that today, under the conditions created by industrialism, the labourer fights a losing battle from the start. The foundation which makes his work the most advantageous of all to him is missing. When society allows the creation of great armies of labourers, without giving to them a shadow of understanding or intellectual compensation, then quite clearly the degeneration of these men into subhuman creatures is inevitable.

The mental worker is hardly better off. He can often be much worse off. Given the spiritual formation to see the purpose and nature of his work, he has perhaps more to offer to God. He cannot contemplate God alone, for that is possible only to the labourer whose mind is free. But he can contemplate some of the things which God is: justice, truth, beauty, order, mercy, and so forth. God is all of these and the contemplation of all of these is the true goal of the intellectual worker.

But he too has his dangers. His physical deterioration is taken for granted, and I wish that that was not regarded as so unimportant. A healthy body is an aid to healthy manhood. By the nature of his mental preoccupation with lesser matters, he is likely to take other things for granted. His natural egotism may distort his standard of values by making some things, chiefly those centred on himself, seem more important than they are. His very faculty for seeing straight is often interfered with by his work. The labourer may ignore God because his vacuous mind is too easily filled with rubbish from outside. The clerk will ignore God because he fills his own mind with things to which he attaches undue importance. I recall a classic instance of a Catholic social worker who was prevented from attending Mass herself by having to prepare a statistical graph of church attendances. If the mind of the clerk is not as straight as an arrow-shaft, it becomes more crooked than he believes possible. If the mind of the labourer is too open, the mind of the

clerk is too closed. His greatest danger is mental confusion. The road to hell is littered with the good inten-
tions of those who believed that being busy about many
things was an adequate substitute for faith. Clear
spiritual direction, constant prayer, and great courage
are needed by the clerk. His work can be noble, but
it can be correspondingly dark.

The most spiritually satisfying of all work is handcraft,
that is, work done by the hands under the direction of
the mind. Truth, in the ordering of matter to God, is
more easily ascertainable. That is, the end of the work
can be more clear. Neither the labourer nor the clerk
can always see the end of their work. Their own particular task may have no visible end, and in order to
relate themselves to the whole, they may have to identify
themselves with the end of the whole organisation. They
may have to see themselves only as units contributing to
a whole. If the end of the whole is futile, invisible, or
valueless, their work is affected adversely. The craftsman, however, can always enjoy a proximate end. The
actual task he does is almost invariably good in that he
is directing the formation of order from chaos. The end
of the whole does not affect him so much, be it a good
end or a bad end. He rarely sees himself simply as a unit.
And he is most exempt from the trade union tendency
to lower standards. The union policy may be the better-
ment of the material conditions of the workmen, but to
achieve this end it usually ignores the nature of the work
to be done, and even actively discourages the idea of
work. The craftsman's task is an exact one; his personal
relation with his work is close. The use of both mind and

body precludes the distraction of one by the demands of the other. The labourer may be exposed to the turbulent demands of a neglected mind and an excited body; the clerk is exposed to the like demands of a neglected body and an excited mind. The craftsman limits the turbulence of both by making a lesser demand on each and by making both demands simultaneously.

Handcraft covers a variety of arts and trades. At the electrical work-bench, I was completely absorbed in work in the company of a number of raffish Cockneys. George the Moron and I could work together shovelling cooked straw, and Bill the Cockney and I could work together assembling circuits. But the most spiritually dynamic work I personally have ever done is wood-carving. Wood-carving calls for a steady hand and a clear mental picture of the finished article. The difficulty with carved lettering is that you cannot rub out a mistake; and cut letters are so stark that a mistake includes the slightest deviation from geometrical symmetry. This is the kind of work that is almost impossible to stop. Mere matters of food, civil strife or thunderbolts never trouble the wood-carver. The sensitiveness with which he must handle his knife is so great that his whole body is ranged behind his tense fingertips. His mind, watching and supervising, never becomes drugged by confusion, because the issue is clear. It cannot relax from its attention to the work, but the image in the mind is as sharp as his knife's blade.

The handcraftsman is the only type of worker whose work helps him to remain sane. He of all workers sells his work rather than himself. In doing so, he is more fully a human person and the nearest thing we have to a fully human worker.

Since it is of the nature of business to turn the craftsman into a labourer, and the labourer into a horse, it follows that the worker may at some point rebel. In its simplest form, this rebellion takes the form of irresponsible behaviour. The well-known parcel-smasher is a typical example. When I worked as a porter, I had to hand parcels to a truck-driver who worked for the railways. He was a great grinning man, who seemed to be happy in his work, and his happiness may have been bought at the price of his conscience: for certainly no parcel was safe in his hands. Those marked "Fragile" were open invitations to him to hurl and kick them into his truck. Rebellion is a consequence of mutilation. Nobody likes to be mutilated.

There is a deeper and less conscious rebellion, however, than the mere kicking and squealing of the reluctant worker. This deeper revolt is the desire for escape by the labourer into the white-collar job. This is not because cuff-and-collar jobs require more of the person than labouring. They do not. If the labourer has been reduced to the status of a horse, the clerk has been reduced to the status of an adding-machine. That both may be noble vocations does not alter the nature of what they generally are. The clerk is no more a whole man than the labourer, but he works in a different atmosphere. He works nearer to the management. Since the state of mind which brought factories into the world also introduced the idea that cleanliness was better than Godliness, the clerk must above all be clean.

In the very phrase "white-collar worker" there is an infinite depth of pathos. When everything has been taken away from the workman that makes him a human being, he can still look like a human being. The lower his humanity falls, the more he can even look like a gentleman. A floor-walker in a department store going to and coming from work is indistinguishable from the managing director.

A proletarian is a man who has sold himself. The white-collar job offers an imitation dignity to the same man clutching for the remnants of his self-respect. It does not take long for the craft worker to envy him too. The craft worker, being a true worker, looks like a worker. Since no one has ever told him about the dignity or integrity of work, he assumes in time that the true dignity of work really is vested in the colour and cut of the fingernails.

If it were not bad enough that men should be obliged to perform work which mutilates their personality, it is worse that men should actually want that form of work which mutilates them most. For the inferiority of the craft worker to the white-collar worker is one of the worst of the lies we have to endure. Jesus was a craftworker. He was not a clerk, a go-between, an agent, or a contact man. He was a renderer into disciplined form of unformed matter, a restorer of order from chaos, a maker of useful chairs from useless wood. Papini sums it up neatly in his Life of Christ.

The craft of Jesus was one of the four most sacred and ancient ones. That of the ploughman, the mason, the carpenter and the smith are, among the manual arts, those most closely connected with the life of man. . . . While the soldier may degenerate into a highwayman, the merchant into an adventurer, the sailor into a pirate, these four cannot change, cannot become corrupt.

Is this incorruptibility of the craft worker clear? Is the divine nobility of such work, in its relation to God, apparent? That which is raw stone, ground by the brutality of nature in a stratum of the earth, can become a statue, a column, a doorstep, a pedestal or an altar. That which is wood in a tree, knotted, twisted and wild, can become a shining crucifix, a table, a hutch, or a handle to turn a butter-churn. The task of bringing the raw materials of nature into line with man's needs, first of survival, and secondly of enrichment and worship, is a way of life that brings man very close to God.

It is in the white-collar occupations, on the other hand, that man dips deepest into degradation. It is easier to prostitute the intellect than it is to prostitute the body. The man whose body is enslaved by the chains of a labour gang can still keep his mind turned upwards. If his mind is turned upwards, it can lift the body with it, and it can turn the worst of manual labour into a divine offering. The clerk's poor body does not work at all. And his mind is turned downwards. The primary skill required is a modest literacy. Upon this the successful clerk builds the secondary skills of glibness, sharpness and conventional observance. The standard of his efficiency is a beaver-like attentiveness to little things—which is the antithesis of the Christian concept of the whole man. There are to be sure some of true skill and wisdom, but these isolated cases are only a minority compared with the mighty horde of typists, "business girls", counters and stampers, office-boys and messengers, minor secretaries, buyers and sellers, human rubber-stamps and elegant arithmeticians, who live in the lowlands of propriety fingering their ties with shy pride and enduring for their sake not only the economic slavery of the common worker, but the social slavery of those who sell out to the god of appearances.

This world of closed offices, of artificial light, of air-conditioning, of surnames politely whispered, of files and filing cabinets, of a million or more human beings jammed like respectable sardines into an area of less than a square mile—this world which battens on the community by buying, selling, insuring, lending, extorting, juggling, cornering, shortening, lengthening, gambling and speculating; this world of so much deceit and hypocrisy is that recommended to the "clever" boy as a goal more worthy of attainment in this life than the perfection of the craft which Jesus Himself practised.

A practical step towards the making of a moron has been taken when a boy who could turn his craft into an art is persuaded by the snobbery of parent or teacher to seek a "better" position in a "respectable" office. I have seen what happened to the men with whom I was at school, men who were told this and who dutifully believed it; the world has lost some great and good men because they did believe it.

All that can be said about the clerks applies with even greater force to the managers. Please take these words carefully, for as I have used the terms "labourer", "craftsman", and "clerk" to describe conveniently a type known to all of us, so do I use "manager". And the problem of the managers is this.

Industrialism began by a minority taking the means of goodness from the majority and applying it to their own corruption. It is a case of the corrupt but strong taking the means of virtue from the vulnerable weak, and thereby corrupting them also. From the ranks of the weak there emerge those whose loss of the way to holiness worries them less than their inability to enjoy the pleasures of a more complete corruption. These members of the oppressed class have the desire, or the ambition, call it what you will, to be as their masters. By accepting the premises on which their own degradation is based they seek favour with their masters; and having won it, they assist their masters in the carrying out of their work. Such are the managers, the foremen, the yes-men, the salaried executives, the stooges, the promising boys with a "good" future. If the generalisation has its exceptions, it is not for that reason alone invalid.

The reward of such servitude is additional chains. The sinister promotions which await the "promising" boy put him in a wretched position. He has all the disadvantages of being a slave without the freedom of a slave. The worst of slaves retain their dignity and their honour and they have a certain curious freedom: the freedom to offer their suffering. The clerk sacrifices part of this freedom, the manager sacrifices all of it. He sacrifices it for the accumulation of material riches; he approves his own oppression for the cheapest of prices. In his pursuit of self, he annihilates soul. For additional pieces of silver, he gives up the vestigial dignity of the poor. And not even those pieces of silver can give him the equality he wants with his employers; he cannot obtain the remotest shadow of the satisfaction he really wants. He can only pretend. He has sought to be as God, but unlike the most ambitious of those who pursue self, the god whom he seeks to be like is only the product of his own delusions.

If this state of affairs were for the natural good of any of the parties—employer, employee, or society—it would still be bad enough. There would at least be precedent for it. But what has happened is this.

The employer has hired bodies to assist him in action. He wishes to act, because he too is a man; his body cries for action, and his soul for order. The concentration into his hands of such enormously increased power for action more than satisfies his bodily craving; it gluts it. He can create, manage and administer in the grand manner. By careful application, he could have a power for the restoration of order, greater than the combined power of himself and his employees as individuals. Is this power so applied to the restoration of order from chaos or of all things to God? No. It is applied to the making of further chaos. The effect of industrial philosophy upon human society has already been shown. The objective of "business" clearly stated in every textbook of economics is the satisfaction of self. The satisfaction of self is the law of the jungle. The existence of the resultant jungle is clear from the effect of industrial philosophy upon human society.

Because the power to act becomes too great, the inclination to order is perverted. That is why the organisation created to execute an ideal usually kills the ideal. The effect is the same as that of offering too great a feast to a wedding guest. He is likely to forget about the wedding. In such a case the passion becomes simply a lust: that is, a powerful desire so capable of part-fulfilment that the good end is forgotten in the immediate satisfaction afforded by the means. An employee by becoming such tends to abandon the better way of integration, partly because of a desire for security, partly through greed, ambition or fear, partly by reason of plain economic pressure. The employer tends to abandon the way of his own integration because the power to act becomes too great. He is diverted to the unsatisfying goal of riches for their own sake. He takes from his employees their means for good and uses them, not for his own good, but for his own corruption.

That is the true evil of proletarianism. It is the true evil of the modern concept of work. We have made the best of a bad thing, just as the paper mill was regarded as a "good" shop for all to work in. But the inherent badness of the thing remains. Marx missed the point because he had only a limited view of man. With so many of his principles now common belief and the turbulence of the proletarian world worse than ever, his error is more clear. A master-servant relationship can be a clean and holy thing, but proletarianism strikes at the very heart of humanity. With its effect upon man's immortal soul we are not directly concerned; but its effect upon his mind and reason, his moral sense and practical judgment leaves us very gloomy.

VIII

THE MAKING OF A MAN

A WORKMAN MUST know what he is doing and do it from free choice. If he knows what he is doing but is not free in his choice, then to the extent of his lack of freedom he is a slave. If his choice is free but he is unaware of the object of his actions, he is either in error or under delusion. In none of these cases can he work well as a man. Knowing what his work is, and freely choosing to do it, he should furthermore be expressing his personality in it. That is, he must make his own judgments as to the execution of it.

Freedom does not mean the absence of all limitation. It means only absence from limitations which frustrate the good end of an action. A workman may be "restricted" by the need for maintaining his family, and by the superior skill and knowledge of his master. Subordination to such factors constitute only the natural boundaries in which freedom can be exercised. Freedom must have boundaries; otherwise it becomes anarchy. There is a lot of anarchy in industry today because workmen do not understand precisely what is meant by freedom.

As between master and servant then, there should exist a relationship of persons. An undesirable feature of industry today is the growth in numbers and size of larger shops where this personal factor cannot exist. Where it does not exist there can only be rules, and the inevitable result is the denial of personality. A retrograde step was the change in concepts from "master" to "boss", for while the master was so because he knew more, the "boss" only owns more. It is unfortunate that the "boss" has now become the "management" or the "system".

The bigger the shop the more rule replaces relationship; but there is one notable exception to the undesirability, from the human point of view, of big organisations. When the function of an organisation possesses integrity, and the carrying out of that function depends essentially upon size, then, in a remarkable way, the personal relationship survives. An army is the best example. An army depends essentially on being big. Size is one of its most important attributes. A formal denial of personality is necessary, and formally the denial is made. Superficially, an army seems to destroy personality more than any other type of organisation. But no man who has ever served in an army will say that it does do so in fact. Size is not of the essence of a paper mill. When size is the product of expansion for no other reason than the value set upon size—size of plant being a factor in size of dividend—then depersonalisation sets in. Size may be essential to certain types of hospital. It is not essential to a store. The effect on the individual is clear in both cases. In the one he remains a person, in the other he becomes only a portion of a man.

It was part of the genius of Marx that he saw, in an age which erected more false standards of value than any other, this fundamental error of working relations. He called it the "class struggle" and assumed that it had always existed. Historically he was wrong but his view of the contemporary scene was right enough. It was morally wrong that only a part of man should be hired, a part paid for, the rest subjected to indignities not inflicted even upon farm animals. But since Marx was not concerned with the soul of man he did not see the real danger.

Work done is the work of a whole man regardless of whether the employer has hired the whole man or not. And since it is fundamental to the dignity of man that he own his work, it is only just that he own it in a more precious way when the whole man is not paid for it. The less of the man actually hired, the more ownership the whole man has of the work actually done. By "owning" his work, I mean that he must do it in his own way, in his own time, and subject to his own conditions. That is, he must have the chance of making a decision himself as to the manner of its execution; he shall not be superintended by stop-watch or time-clock, but shall exercise his own judgment as to the time it takes to complete the work; and the series of judgments involved in the execution of the work, including the ultimate judgment—that of passing the act of judgment to another—shall be his. This is of course subject to rational qualifications which are implicit in the word "judgment". There are skill variations, implicit and explicit authorities, obvious occasions of co-operation, and terms of contract. The fact still remains that it is his work.

An example of the unfortunate attitude adopted by some "masters"—in this case, an under-manager—was the order to work faster. This is the kind of remark addressed to a farm animal which has an inclination to avoid work altogether. A man craves work because he is human. The differences that are in men are the joy of the human race, and some will work faster, some slower, some better and some worse. Human beings are not animals.

There cannot be fear for, if there is, the freedom of choice is impeded. Fear exists on all levels, at present, and its effects are most noticeable in the managerial class. Since it is founded mainly on the insecurity of the servant, it can only be avoided by the granting of presumptive rights of ownership in a business. This is a controversial matter, and requires careful explanation.

If a master engages a servant, he does so on the basis of contract between them. In the case of a written or explicit contract, the question does not arise. In the case of an implied contract the terms are more difficult to ascertain. The wage payment can be defined in exact terms, and is; but the quality or quantity of work cannot, and over a period of time a good and satisfactory workman tends to give the employer more than he actually contracted for. I have heard employers on many occasions complaining that their staff do no more than the least asked of them. The answer, of course, is that the employer never pays more than the least he stipulated. Employers, almost universally, expect the whole man to be placed at their disposal. Their aggrieved attitude is often quite sincere when a workman insists on fulfilling no more than the terms of the contract. Yet it is obvious: if a servant is a good servant, he has brought more of his whole personality to the task. He is giving the employer parts of him which the employer has not contracted to pay for. He gives him loyalty, interest, intelligence, inventiveness, and imagination. There is more genuine justice in the employer who says, though sometimes impolitely, that such things are not required from the servant, than in the employer who accepts these gifts as marks only of a "satisfactory" servant.

In return the good servant may get nothing. The master may recognise the injustice of the minimum contract by way of bonus or gift, but as these come literally as gifts, there is no justice in that. For all that he gives to the business, the good servant may get nothing that alters his status as a servant. What can he get?

Since length of service is the best criterion of good service, it follows that long service should bring a man certain rights of ownership. The business becomes partly his. He cannot be dismissed at the boss's whim, and the boss cannot impose policies with which the good servant is at variance. It is unjust that the whole of a good servant's life should be spent in fear of becoming more dependent on his master, as he does simply by growing older, instead of each becoming more mutually dependent on the other.

This relationship is often reached accidentally, but in the absence of a rule, it is itself open to serious abuse. A servant can assume powers which a master is forced to recognise. In the absence of an acknowledgment of the servant's actual position, the temptation for the good servant to become a bad servant is very strong. In a well-known London cafeteria chain, the waiters and waitresses, who were always in a state of war with the management, held one useful trump against injustice. If one of their number was ill-treated, the time for some or all to strike or resign was during the lunch-time rush-hour. The sudden disappearance of staff, even of one or two, during this critical period threw the whole cafeteria into chaos, and the management as a result had been firmly disciplined into treating their staff with some outward respect. But it goes further than that. A servant with a knowledge of the master's business, who yet lives in any fear of the master's authority over him, invariably has a moral struggle. Nobody who has not had the experience can understand what it is like to know that one is grossly underpaid, and at the same time to be handling the master's books and accounts. It is common sense from the master's viewpoint, as well as justice from the servant's, that the unpaid-for contribution of the good servant should be acknowledged, his independence increased, and his proprietary interest in the business recognised. Not only his ownership of his work, but his partnership in the business is essential to his proper functioning as a man.

The only qualification to this is that the master must retain the right to protect the quality of his work. As master, he directs the quality of it. The more he himself has raised and established the standard of that work, the more he is entitled to protect it. So that the presumptive right which an employee has in a business can never extend to any aspect of that business to which he has not made his unpaid-for contribution. Clearly the slow-witted assistant of an artisan gains no rights in the nature of the work done by mere length of service; especially when such length of service is marked by sheer inability to rise beyond the initial laborious duties for which one was engaged. But that same slow-witted assistant, who may do nothing more than sweep and clean, is protected by justice in his job as sweeper and cleaner, becomes the owner so to speak of the sweeping-and-cleaning aspect of the business, and must be confirmed in his rights as a partner to dictate policy on sweeping-and-cleaning to the man who is ostensibly his master. Again this position is often reached accidentally. The king's stable-boy may very well dictate policy on the king's horse to the king himself. If the king interferes with this, if he draws upon his other authority to oblige the stable-boy to a course of action which the latter in conscience finds repellent to him, the king is rightly regarded as a bully and a tyrant. But this frequent accidental recognition of rights is not sufficient. The dignity of the workman demands more than a genial acknowledgment of an existing state of affairs. The relationship should be acknowledged formally.

The restoration of all things to God can in some instances be a complex matter, and beyond the powers of even the most normal or energetic man in the fullness of his intellect and strength. The task may need to be broken down into several operations, each the responsibility of a man whom we call a specialist. Specialisation is a by-product of complexity, and with the growing complexity of in-dustrial operations there are a variety of operations which only a chain of workmen can do. I remember a woman aircraft-worker telling me, during the war, how thrilled she was whenever she saw one of "her" planes fly past. Her particular job was only a minor piece of tail assembly, but it was wartime, and she was the wife of an airman. Beaufighter bombers do not seem directly intended to restore anything to God, but in her mind there was a motive in making, clearly related to the whole view of work. Specialisation has two opposing objects. On the one hand it enables work to be done better by encouraging an increase in skill in a chain of individual craftsmen. Just as a surgeon may specialise on the brain, so a motor mechanic may specialise on carburetters. On the other hand, specialisation can be the substitution for craftsmen of an assembly line of simplified operations. The motive for specialisation in the former case is the encouraging of the intellect in its exploration of the mysteries of matter; in the latter case, the discouraging of the intellect from any exploration at all. By being thus denied the access of the individual intellect to work, human beings are turned into working animals. Instead of six brains and six pairs of hands combining to produce a better creation, one brain and a dozen pair of hands produce what is only a more profitable creation.

This form of specialisation is one of the fastest ways of making a moron out of a man. By definition a smaller part still of the whole man is used. The assembly line experts are constantly seeking simpler and smaller processes, so that they can use less and less of whole men. More and more men are used in decreasing quotas of humanity each. The worker is less and less concerned with what he is doing, he sees no origin or end to it, he gets no guidance or stimulus to work. He works for the moment and in an endless sequence of moments.

The less of the whole man employed on the job, the more dangerously turbulent becomes that part of him which is not being used. Action produces reaction and industrial unrest is the outcome. There is never more unrest anywhere than in a community of well-fed, well-organised, hygienically housed process workers. If there is no unrest, then God alone can help them, for it means they have thrown in the towel. The soul of man does not want to be degraded in comfort. It does not want to be degraded at all. The more "conditions of work" are improved, the more hot showers, rest-rooms, cafeterias, armchairs, or music-while-you-work provided, the more revolting to the soul of man the system becomes.

This is the tragic bedrock of "big business". The bigger the shop, in terms of economic "efficiency", the more it tends to utilise less and less of the man. It wants only a part of him; his strength, his senses, his voice, his literacy. It throws away the rest of him. The impersonalised monster of a master requires only impersonalised minutiae of men.

It has already gone so far that a large number of men are irredeemable. They have been dehumanised, they have become morons, and they will never work well again. Although the fury of men today who find so many work-men untrustworthy, unreliable and uncertain is understandable, the workmen themselves have a point of view. Give them a master who is prepared to grant to them all the just conditions of work, and they will regard him —having being trained to do so—as a simpleton to be cheated. A moron, after all, who is treated by a kindly person as a fully developed human being will soon take advantage of his new position.

I do not see the answer to this problem. There are workmen left in the world who yearn to be treated as men; there are others who have forgotten that they are men. The distinction must be left to the individual good employer, and there is a challenge to the good employer, by a mixture of firm discipline and warm love, to restore the manhood of those who have lost it. Just as a delinquent may be brought slowly back to the life of virtue, or a moron may be slowly trained to a higher form of life, so the abandoned workman may, at the hands of a good employer, return to a realisation of his true nature. That is a task for the isolated, and necessarily courageous good employer. But the good employer will have to fight not only the abandoned worker himself, but the industrial world as well. The making of morons by big industry means that the time is coming, if it has not already arrived, when of any two men seeking the same employment, the one with the lesser intelligence will be preferred to the one with the greater. Man is marching to the employment offered by precisely those forms of industry where the whole man has least chance of survival. The process of centralisation and simplification is constant. Since the whole man must be on the job, he must inevitably become a restless revolutionary, a moron, or a saint. The last mentioned is by far the rarest. The number of revolutionaries is still ominously small, and though they must, in their own way, cause trouble, an increase in their numbers would at least show that the true spirit of man was managing to survive.

The employer, the rich man, the man of property and power, has a different problem if he is to remain a man or regain his manhood. His problem is that too many goods, too many opportunities, too many powers divert him from reality. At one end of the scale, the workman loses contact with reality by losing parts of his self; at the other end the man of property and power loses contact with reality by having too many additional parts to his self. There is a norm somewhere, and since no man sits exactly at either of these too extremes, the problems of the man of property will help the poor man too. They are both men. They are both poor in some things and they are both rich in others.

Preoccupation with self is the essence of mental disease of all sorts. The highest and noblest form of man is the man who has risen furthest from the demands of self. As the stature of man decreases, so can be observed a retreat into the contemplation of self: the desire *to be* descends into the desire *to seem*; and from there into the desire *to have*; the lowest level of so-called normality is the man whose only surviving contact with reality is with the physical reality of his self. The next step down is the contemplation of more restricted aspects of his self—his stomach, or his sexual passions; and still lower down there is the preoccupation with an unreal self which is the sign of the clinically diagnosable lunatic.

Material possessions—including, in that term, powers, skills, and abilities and propensities—fall into two readily recognisable categories: those which are tools and those which are toys. Do not be misled by the simplicity of the terms. A tool is something which aids a man's work. A toy is something which diverts him from reality and turns his mind to a world of make-believe, in which he is the central figure. Children are not the only people with a great desire for toys; and we allow children to have toys only because they must be broken into reality gently.

Man must work, and in addition he must also love God and his neighbour. The virtue of charity and the necessity for working can be fitted together in the matter of restoring all things to God. Work is necessary in the restoring of order from chaos in matter; work is also the exercise of charity in the restoring of order from chaos among men. Work and charity go together. That is why work so-called which is solely concerned with the satisfaction of self ultimately reduces man to a low level of being.

In order to work well, tools may be necessary. A tool is not only a hammer or a chisel. We have restricted the meaning of the word. A tool includes a doctor's car as well as his stethoscope, a serviceable swivel-chair for an administrator, an inkwell for a journalist, a tongue for a lecturer, a sitting-room for a housewife, a bowl of flowers for a hostess, a panelled wall for a king. All the things which help the work of a man are tools. Since a man has, whether he likes it or not, a station in life in which he works, the things which help him to maintain that station are equally tools by nature. All these words, even such as "station in life" need exact definition. "Station in life" means only that level at which our work is best done. If the custom of society requires that a lawyer wear a black suit, that suit is a tool of trade. If the custom of society requires an artist to wear a corduroy jacket and long hair, those too are tools of trade. Professional and trade groups still retain their customs and uniforms. The office-boy who dresses like an artist is obviously more concerned with self, more concerned with seeming, than he is with fulfilling his true nature as an office-boy. A certain prudence, a certain rational judgment and knowledge of the fitness of things, must qualify some of these apparently wide generalisations.

The normal object of man in this life is the service of God by prayer, work and charity. For these three activities, tools are necessary, and it follows that since there is precious little time for, or sense in, doing anything else, no other goods are required but tools. For the only other goods we can have are toys, things which help us to forget reality, things which we contemplate for their own sake, and the effect of which is to turn our contemplation inwards towards self. Such goods restrict our freedom by taking our attention from more important things. Energy which is all too little for the main task, is diverted to the end of immediate and transient self-satisfaction.

Let us again be prudent. A man may use possessions for the purpose of relaxation, rest and legitimate enjoyment. The proportions must be observed. Recreation, the re-creation of man after the wastage caused by fatigue, the restoration of the man himself after the dissipation of his powers, is essential to his life. Rest and enjoyment may be most essential contributions to work; and if they are, then what may seem to be toys become, in an indirect way, his tools. I foresee the danger here of being mistaken for a stern puritan who would grind the nose of man into work to the exclusion of love, laughter and beauty. I do not want to do that, for love, laughter and beauty, in their right proportion, are essential to man.

Take the case of a magnetic wire recorder. To a free-lance producer of plays, such a costly instrument is a valuable tool of trade. The sensitivity with which it can record sound, be it voices or music, and the ease with which that sound can be returned in another place at a different time, mixed with other sounds, makes it a very useful tool for doing better work. In one's occasionally less responsible moments, the same costly instrument may be used for the lightest and most trivial of pranks or pleasures. One cannot stand in judgment and say that the use of the instrument here or there is right or wrong. But one can say that a rich man, whose house is already loaded with possessions reflecting his earthly glory, who buys such a thing for his daughter's birthday for the sheer novelty of pranks and pleasure only is wasting his money and his time, and displaying a very childish sense of values by using it for such.

Possessions which are not necessary tools of good living extend and enlarge a man's attachment to this life and to himself. His preoccupation with little things leads him naturally to the preoccupation with himself, the smallest thing he knows. A man should not possess goods, powers or skills which turn his mind in and downwards. They do him no good.

The world however teaches man, by its various methods of indoctrination, that the more he possesses, the "better" man he is. Possessions have taken on a value of their own. They are revered, even worshipped, for their own sake. The accumulation of real and personal property, from knick-knacks to landed estates, for no other purpose than the glorification of the owner, is the accepted standard of success. "A man of property" is a man commanding prestige in the eyes of this world. Ownership is a robe of excellence among the men who applaud the doctrine of self-supremacy. This form of idolatry can be seen in many of the sumptuous houses of rich men, and to a worse degree in middle-class maisonettes. It is primitive behaviour, restricting the freedom of man to act at all, and restricting certainly the opportunity for directing his attention to the necessary things.

The excellence of tools, however, can give them a certain toy-value, which may distract from their primary function. Modesty is a much abused virtue, but it means only that a thing should be appropriate and serviceable. A large diamond tie-pin can be the most immodest of things: a larder necessary to give hospitality is a necessary tool of charity, but an over-stocked liquor cupboard which does not reflect the charity of its owner but only advertises his wealth is also immodest. Immodest things, tools which have become toys, are those things we usually call by more popular words such as "ostentatious", "vulgar", or "pretentious". An immodest thing is a gilded lily, a thing carrying too much evidence of its lesser purposes, and thereby being lessened as to its major object. Tools of work and living have many degrees of efficiency and splendour. The splendour which follows utility is a natural reflection of God. The splendour which exists for its own sake is a natural reflection of self. When splendour interferes with utility, then of course the tool should be discarded as a toy in disguise. Motor-cars are often toys in disguise.

The possession of wealth acquired through work is simply the possession of more powerful tools and implements for work and charity; and to whom much is given of him much is expected. As a person's fortune in worldly things seems to grow, as his wealth increases disproportionately to the effort he has made, so more and more is expected in the way of restoring all things to God. The man who is rich without having to work at all owes most; and the biggest of all damned fools is the man who is rich without work, and who turns this wealth entirely over to the ritual worship of self.

A man does not need riches. Unless they be immediately diverted to the service of others, riches soften a man until he is like a jelly, both physically and mentally.

A man does not need security. God has promised that man will be given what he needs for his most important end, and it is presumptuous of man to forget that end by a morose preoccupation with merely local problems of security.

A man does not need comfort. A baby needs comforting because it is not yet in touch with reality. But a man functions better as a man if his body is disciplined, hardened and steeled. He needs spiritual truth and knowledge of his purpose and, if he has those, he does not even feel the need for comfort.

THE MAKING OF A MAN

A man does not need to avoid suffering. Nor does he need soporifics, dopes, escapist satisfactions to help him dodge natural suffering. It is common experience that those who suffer reach the highest level of nobility when they know why they are suffering and if they accept it as a necessary part of a small price to pay for a great prize.

A man must work; and work includes a struggle, a battle with nature and with self. No man who claims to be a man will avoid battle.. The dragon fought by St. George is met by every man. The dragon is around us all the time, and his chaos must be met, and defeated. It is impossible to fight a dragon without emerging scarred and breathless. That is the least a man can expect.